PRAISE FOR *BREAKTHROUGH LEADERSHIP IN THE DIGITAL AGE*

by Frederick M. Hess and Bror Saxberg

Hess and Saxberg offer a powerful read for principals as the chief "learning engineers" in schools. Instructional leaders know that technology has changed the complexion of schools and classrooms, but their leadership is needed to steward its use to solve learning challenges.

Principals are becoming masters of navigating programs, gadgets, and curricula to best utilize resources. Applying the principles of learning science to these leadership competencies will deepen the level of thinking about technology, and lead to more meaningful student outcomes.

By deconstructing learning science and making the connection to technology, the authors have outlined key strategies for school leaders as they work to transform traditional practices in schools. The insights and ideas put forth by Hess and Saxberg will help principals implement myriad practices that fully realize the potential of technology and digital learning.

Whether it is whole-school reform or targeted interventions, principals will be motivated to rethink or "re-engineer" the use of technology to optimize teaching and learning.

Gail Connelly
Executive Director, National Association of Elementary School Principals
Alexandria, VA

Hess and Saxberg cut through the ed-tech hype and identify great instruction as the key to improved learning outcomes. Teachers, as well as school and district leaders, will find in these pages an effective blueprint for trying and deploying instructional technologies that is at once deeply conceptual and entirely practical.

Stacey Childress
Deputy Director, Innovation
Seattle, WA

Breakthrough Leadership in the Digital Age provides clear insights and thoughtful design to help schools understand that the main thing with technology is not the technology; it is what you do with it. The authors provide a powerful example vital to the understanding of creating classrooms that are full of "learning engineers" including teachers and students.

Mark Edwards
Superintendent, Mooresville Graded School District
Mooresville, NC

"Learning engineering," the application of learning science to learning at scale, is likely to be a critical ingredient to make progress in online and on-the-ground education in the years to come. The use of technology in education is finally fulfilling its potential. Bror and Rick are leading thinkers in this accelerating space.

Salman Khan
Founder and Executive Director, Khan Academy
Mountain View, CA

It's not the tools, as Rick and Bror point out; it's the new potential to engineer engaging pathways to mastery, to leveraging great technology and buying time for teachers to build powerful sustained relationships with young people. Rick's attention to "cage-busting leadership" and Bror's relentless demand for learning R&D make them great coauthors—and make this a must read.

Tom Vander Ark
Author and CEO, Getting Smart
Federal Way, WA

The democratization of information and the availability of technology are two of the biggest issues facing American public education today and can have a transformative impact on teaching and learning. But we can't simply plug new devices into old classrooms. In *Breakthrough Leadership in the Digital Age*, Hess and Saxberg make it clear that we can only fully leverage the educational possibilities of technology if we are willing to become "learning engineers" first, and redesign our schools, classrooms, and teaching practices to take full advantage of these tools. This will require bold leadership and dramatic changes to the way we structure our school day, train our educators, and deliver instruction. This book is an important part of the conversation about what it means to education children in the 21st century.

Joshua P. Starr, EdD
Superintendent, Montgomery County Public Schools
Rockville, MD

The concept of a "learning engineer" is nothing short of an overdue revolution in thinking about innovation in public education. Leaders across the educator sector, who are committed to improvement in service to kids, must resist the silver bullet promise of shiny new tools air-dropped into yesterday's classrooms. Hess and Saxberg tell us why, and more importantly, how to squarely place people as the drivers of innovation. The pragmatic approach laid out in this book will help leaders recognize that kids need more than touch screens. They need teachers, school and district leaders, and policymakers who approach this work as entrepreneurial problem finders, thoughtfully applying technology as a solution when and where it makes sense.

Jennifer Medberry
CEO, Kickboard
New Orleans, LA

Technology alone will not improve teaching or learning in our schools. However, as Hess and Saxberg have succinctly laid out, if leveraged properly by effective educators, technology can and will have a profound impact on the educational landscape. It is important that all education stakeholders embrace this way of thinking in order to effectively move technology use in schools beyond just quantity of devices to quality of learning experiences.

Josh Stumpenhorst
2012 Illinois Teacher of the Year
Naperville, IL

This is a "must-read" book for educational leaders, policymakers, educational product developers and those of us who have a stake in our education system. While many books have described ways that educational technology can help save our K–12 education system, this book is different. Hess and Saxberg combine a realistic view of technology with an engaging and accurate description of what we know about learning sciences and a discussion about how to combine the two. Their concern is that technology is often a solution in search of a problem to solve—a solution that seems very seldom to bring expected benefits. They remind us with brief cautionary stories that different technologies are empty vehicles that are most often used to deliver educational products whose impact has ranged from destructive to ineffective—but also that occasionally their impact is positive and game-changing. They describe many popular but failed approaches that should be avoided because of solid evidence that they don't work. They also offer compelling examples to support their view that the best outcomes occur when forward-thinking school leaders combine solid, evidence-based learning strategies chosen to solve identified problems, with cost-effective technology. They describe the strategies they recommend. They offer clear and specific pointers about how to use these learning science based strategies and an engineering approach to create smart school reform (with and without technology).

Richard E. Clark
Professor Emeritus of Educational Psychology and Technology;
Co-Director of the Center for Cognitive Technology; and
Clinical Professor of Surgery, University of Southern California
Los Angeles, CA

As we educators expect our children to think deeply and critically about the world around them, we should expect nothing less of ourselves. Here, Rick and Bror provide us with an outline for that thinking. They push us to ask the right questions as we challenge the conventional approaches to learning within our schools. This book is about far more than educational technology; it is a call to critical thought from an orientation that aims first and foremost to provide excellent learning opportunities for our children.

Mark T. Murphy
Secretary of Education,
Delaware Department of Education
Dover, DE

This important book urges readers to create powerful, new learning environments based on learning science. Technology can be transformative when we focus on actual learning experiences and not just the shiniest gadget.

Alex Hernandez
Charter School Growth Fund
Broomfield, CO

This is a great "how to" book for any district that is interested in tackling the technology challenges for our students. It gives a new way to think about instructional delivery and how to best prepare ourselves for facilitating learning in the 21st Century.

Colleen Jones
Assistant Superintendent for
Academic Services, Liberty Public Schools
Liberty, MO

Hess and Saxberg are spot-on about the right future for the role of science and technology in education. They wonderfully combine an enthusiasm for new and creative approaches with a clear-minded "does it really work?" skepticism. This book presents the most clear argument I have seen that learning science can make a huge difference in improving student learning and lowering costs.

Ken Koedinger
Professor of Human-Computer Interaction
and Psychology, Carnegie Mellon University
Pittsburgh, PA

Hess & Saxberg recognize that thoughtful use of technology in schools is not primarily technical nor technological—rather, it is human. Or, as the old cartoon character Pogo said, I have seen the enemy, and it is me. *Breakthrough Leadership in the Digital Age* is a must-read for education leaders who want to harness the possibility of new tools, and do so in a thoughtful way that makes a difference for learning.

Keith Krueger
CEO, Consortium for School Networking (CoSN)
Washington, DC

This book provides powerful insight into why state, civic, and system leaders should rethink policies, practices, and procedures related to technology and its usage in our classrooms. Too often, our current structures fail to promote and support learning engineering. Rick Hess and Bror Saxberg have designed a compelling guide for the road ahead.

William Hite
Superintendent, School District of Philadelphia
Philadelphia, PA

Breakthrough Leadership in the Digital Age

Using Learning Science to Reboot Schooling

Frederick M. Hess

Bror Saxberg

CORWIN
A SAGE Company

CORWIN
A SAGE Company

FOR INFORMATION:

Corwin

A SAGE Company

2455 Teller Road

Thousand Oaks, California 91320

(800) 233-9936

www.corwin.com

SAGE Publications Ltd.

1 Oliver's Yard

55 City Road

London EC1Y 1SP

United Kingdom

SAGE Publications India Pvt. Ltd.

B 1/I 1 Mohan Cooperative Industrial Area

Mathura Road, New Delhi 110 044

India

SAGE Publications Asia-Pacific Pte. Ltd.

3 Church Street

#10-04 Samsung Hub

Singapore 049483

Copyright © 2014 by Corwin

Photo Credits

Pages 19 and 20: Used with permission from Carpe Diem Schools.

Pages 102 and 104: Used with permission from Mooresville Graded School District.

Pages 129 and 130: Used with permission from Rocketship Education.

Pages 156 and 157: Used with permission from Summit Public Schools.

Printed in the United States of America

A catalog record of this book is available from the Library of Congress.

ISBN 978-1-4522-5549-1

This book is printed on acid-free paper.

Acquisitions Editor: Arnis Burvikovs

Associate Editor: Desirée A. Bartlett

Editorial Assistant: Ariel Price

Production Editor: Amy Schroller

Copy Editor: Dan Gordon

Typesetter: C&M Digitals (P) Ltd.

Proofreader: Caryne Brown

Indexer: Maria Sosnowski

Cover Designer: Bryan Fishman

Certified Chain of Custody

SUSTAINABLE FORESTRY INITIATIVE

Promoting Sustainable Forestry

www.sfiprogram.org

SFI-01268

SFI label applies to text stock

13 14 15 16 17 10 9 8 7 6 5 4 3 2 1

Contents

Preface

Years ago, one of us attended an information session for virtual charter school parents. At the end, one mother, who had waited until everyone else asked their questions, walked up with her teenage son. He wore a baseball cap, slouchy jeans, and a smile. After checking to ensure that no one was near, she said quietly, "My boy is slow. It takes him the longest time to understand things. He works and works and works at it, and he does get it, eventually, but it sure takes a long time." She looked down, then up: "Is my boy going to be all right?"

That's a profound question: What does it take to ensure that learners of all kinds are going to be "all right"? We think today there are too many schools and classrooms where we can't confidently assuage that mother's fears. What fills us with optimism is that we think there are emerging tools and classroom models that, if used *wisely*, will make it much more likely that we'll be able to tell millions more parents the words they yearn to hear.

The truth is that helping all children master skills and knowledge, whatever their challenges and needs, requires an amount of time, practice, reinforcement, and customization that is simply not feasible in most conventional schools and classrooms—especially in an era of tight budgets. Emerging technological tools, however, make it newly possible to practically and affordably offer those very things to untold millions of children . . . if school and system leaders know what they're doing.

Consider Acton Academy in Austin, Texas. A tiny, independent school with just about 30 students, Acton looks radically different from most schools in Austin, or anywhere else. Students set their own learning goals, plan their own days, and manage their own time. They aren't separated into grades because the school's founders Laura and Jeff Sandefer believe children benefit from working alongside multi-aged peers. Students learn content and assess their progress using technology-enhanced materials offered by the likes of Khan Academy, DreamBox Learning, and ST Math. The school faculty includes one master teacher and two "assistants" (typically high school volunteers earning class credit).[1] The teacher operates as more of a guide than a guru. With the aid of Acton's 11-month academic year, students get all the time they need to master things—and learn at a pace and in a manner geared to help ensure that they're going to be "all right." As Caroline Vander Ark, chief operating officer at Getting Smart, observed after a visit: "Very little teaching took place during my visit, but there was a lot of learning."[2] Acton has reported some promising results, with students gaining more than two grade levels per year on the SAT 10.[3]

In short, many who fret about the baleful impact of education technology have long championed schools like Acton—small, differentiated, student-centered, and rich in personal interactions. Acton is a tiny school, but it stands as one tiny example of what's possible if educators free themselves to rethink the 19th century schoolhouse. Acton shows skeptics that technology can indeed play a role in moving a school forward. This book is intended for those open to bringing that same kind of rethinking to a much broader canvas.

Unfortunately, it sometimes seems that many tech cheerleaders are suggesting that new technology will inevitably improve learning, save money, startle young minds, and solve our edu-problems all by itself. They tout a series of cool new gizmos and notions—like smartphones apps, iPads for all students, "flipped" classrooms, "big data," computer-based instruction, game-based learning—and seemingly suggest that we should just get out of the way. To educators, it can sound as if they're supposed to just head down to the Apple store, fill their backpacks with new gadgets, and call it a day. Given this state of affairs, it's no surprise that educators are often skeptical of new devices and the proselytizers who pitch them.

We want to be painfully clear. We believe that there *is* tremendous potential in new educational technology, but unless it is wielded wisely and well, most of this stuff will amount to no more than a costly, faddish fling with distracting devices. Today, while schools increasingly have remarkable tools at their disposal, we fear these are rarely wielded wisely or well. We're using iPad hammers to open learning paint cans—pursuing poor solutions to the wrong problems.

It's a mistake to get caught up in the question, "Is technology good or bad?" We don't think this makes any more sense than asking whether pencils and books are "good or bad," or whether a doctor's stethoscope and X-ray are "good or bad." These things are tools, and the value of a tool lies in how it is used. The question that motivates *this* book is, "Given what we know about learning, how can new technological tools help promote great teaching and learning?"

The good news and the bad news about technology and learning are one and the same: Schools have not yet begun to systematically tap learning science through technology to deepen, accelerate, and nurture learning. The "bad" here is obvious. So what's the "good" news? It's that, since we mostly haven't figured out the right way to put things together, we're in a position to make enormous progress by tapping emerging tools and technologies the right way.

As we'll suggest in the pages ahead, learning science is the proper starting point for tapping that potential. Acton Academy, like so many other promising pilots over the decades, can succeed with its tiny population by relying on little more than imagination, pluck, and improvisation. But finding ways to mirror that success in schools and systems that serve thousands or tens of thousands of students requires something more. Learning science provides the grounding, insight, and knowledge to inform that work.

Setting this in motion requires educational leaders to start thinking more like "learning engineers," using learning science to inform decisions about what teachers should do and how schools and classrooms should be designed. While there's a wealth of research exploring how the human mind learns, relatively little of it has been used to inform decisions about how to rethink schools and systems. Whether this is because the findings are encrypted within jargon-laden journals, are too new to have migrated to training, or are outside the expertise of those who train and mentor school leaders, it's time to start remedying the situation.

This is a book for problem-solving educators who are unwilling to simply plug new tools into yesterday's classrooms and who want some help when it comes to designing new ways to better serve kids. In our experience, this "learning engineer" mind-set does not always come naturally to education leaders who have spent their entire careers in familiar routines; it will require a reboot.

For starters, it's important to note that good engineers are not technicians. They are creative spirits who find ways to use available talent, time, tools, technology, processes, and underpinning science to solve important problems. Technology has the unique promise of taking great solutions and making them more affordable, available, reliable, personalized, and data-rich. But it has to be used correctly and intentionally.

Today's educational leaders are in a place where they can drive school redesign by tapping into what is known about how minds learn, while using technology as a tool to support and empower these efforts. In this book we hope to help educators and education leaders eager to start thinking more like learning engineers, and offer guidance on how they might best use the power of technology to create the schools and systems our children deserve.

With that, let's see what we can do to help ensure that millions more parents can be confident that their children are "going to be all right."

NOTES

1. Clayton Christensen Institute. (2013). Acton Academy blended learning profiles. Retrieved from http://www.christenseninstitute.org/acton-academy-2/
2. Vander Ark, C. (2012). It's all about culture at Acton Academy. [Weblog post]. Retrieved from http://gettingsmart.com/cms/blog/2012/10/its-all-about-culture-acton-academy/
3. Staker, H. C. (2012). The first principle of blended learning. [Weblog post]. Clayton Christensen Institute. Retrieved from http://wpdev.designfarm.com/cci/the-first-principle-of-blended-learning/

Acknowledgments

W e owe an enormous debt of gratitude to those who provided the guidance, insight, and support that made this volume possible. First and foremost, we'd like to offer our heartfelt thanks to the marvelously talented Taryn Hochleitner for her inspiring work ethic and deft editorial touch. Without Taryn's firm guidance we're not sure this book would have come to fruition.

This is a book informed by the wisdom of those doing work in the field. We owe thanks to all those who made time to talk to us or advised us along the way. Special thanks are due to Dick Clark of the University of Southern California for his willingness to be a supportive sounding board and guide to the wide world of learning science. We also want to thank the terrific team at Corwin, especially Senior Acquisitions Editor Arnis Burvikovs for his friendship, support, and thoughtful guidance, along with Ariel Price, Editorial Assistant, and Amy Schroller, Project Editor.

As ever, Rick owes the deepest appreciation to the American Enterprise Institute and its president, Arthur Brooks, for the remarkable support and steadfast backing that make it possible to pursue this work. He also wishes to thank Taryn's colleagues Lauren Aronson, KC Deane, Max Eden, Andrew Kelly, Daniel Lautzenheiser, Michael McShane, and Jenna Talbot for their invaluable support throughout this project. The authors also owe a vote of thanks to interns Chelsea Straus, Sarah Baran, and Luke Sullivan.

Rick is also indebted to his wife, Joleen, for her love, understanding, and droll editorial support, things that helped carry him through this project as they have through so many others. And he owes big thanks to his loving dad, Milton Hess, for years of insights and anecdotes that helped him better understand the world of information technology.

On the professional front, thanks from Bror are due to Andy Rosen, CEO of Kaplan, whose thoughtful approach to business success through better learning provides a great platform for learning engineers to make a difference. Bror also has a real appreciation for the pioneering work of the business leaders and learning engineers throughout Kaplan who are building a base of practice and evidence that is putting the principles in this book to work at scale. Thanks are due to Bror's own team within Kaplan, especially Brenda Sugrue, David Niemi, and Amelia Waters, for the good but intense work of guiding Kaplan's progress in learning, and Kimberly Hayes, his assistant, for the nearly-as-difficult work of guiding him.

On the personal front for Bror, his parents, Borje and Aase, successfully survived his youth and have given him practical examples of the benefits of supporting deliberate practice, not "smarts," throughout his life. Bror's kids, Haakon, Siri, and Tor, have given him three of the best reasons in the world to think hard about investing in people's learning and their long-term success. Thanks and love from Bror go to his ever-patient wife Denise, who has found so many ways to give their family all the support they need to become what they intend.

Finally, it goes without saying that any mistakes or flaws are ours and ours alone, while most of the good stuff was inevitably cribbed from one of the aforementioned. But such is life.

PUBLISHER'S ACKNOWLEDGMENTS

Corwin gratefully acknowledges the contributions of the following reviewers:

Alex Hernandez, Partner
Charter School Growth Fund
Broomfield, CO

Michael B. Horn, Education Executive Director
Clayton Christensen Institute for Disruptive Innovation
San Mateo, CA

Colleen Jones, Assistant Superintendent for Academic Services
Liberty Public Schools
Liberty, MO

Dr. Jadi Miller, Director of Curriculum and Professional Development
Lincoln Public Schools
Lincoln, NE

Brigitte Tennis, Headmistress and 8th Grade Teacher
Stella Schola Middle School
Redmond, WA

About the Authors

An educator, political scientist and author, **Frederick M. Hess** studies K–12 and higher education issues as the director of education policy studies at the American Enterprise Institute. His books include *Cage-Busting Leadership, The Same Thing Over and Over, Education Unbound, Common Sense School Reform, Revolution at the Margins,* and *Spinning Wheels.* He is also the author of the popular *Education Week* blog, "Rick Hess Straight Up." Hess's work has appeared in scholarly and popular outlets such as *Teachers College Record, Harvard Education Review, Social Science Quarterly, Urban Affairs Review, American Politics Quarterly, The Chronicle of Higher Education, Phi Delta Kappan, Educational Leadership, U.S. News & World Report, National Affairs,* the *Atlantic, National Review,* the *Washington Post,* the *Wall Street Journal,* and the *New York Times.* He has edited widely cited volumes on education philanthropy, school costs and productivity, the impact of education research, and No Child Left Behind. Hess serves as executive editor of *Education Next,* as lead faculty member for the Rice Education Entrepreneurship Program, and on the review boards for the Broad Prize in Urban Education and the Broad Prize for Public Charter Schools. He also serves on the boards of directors of the National Association of Charter School Authorizers and 4.0 Schools. A former high school social studies teacher, he has taught at the University of Virginia, the University of Pennsylvania, Georgetown University, Rice University, and Harvard University. He holds an MA and PhD in government, as well as an MEd in teaching and curriculum, from Harvard University.

 **Bror Saxberg** is responsible for the research and development of innovative learning strategies, technologies, and products across Kaplan's full range of educational services offerings, focused on lifting learner success. He also oversees future developments and adoptions of innovative learning technologies and works to maintain consistent academic standards for Kaplan's products and courses.

Saxberg formerly served as senior vice president and chief learning officer at K12, Inc., where he was responsible for designing both online and off-line learning environments and developing new student products and services. Prior to joining K12, Inc., he was vice president at Knowledge Universe, where he cofounded the testing and assessment division that became known as Knowledge Testing Enterprise (KTE). Saxberg began his career at McKinsey & Company, Inc., and later served as vice president and general manager for London-based DK Multimedia, part of DK Publishing, an education and reference publisher.

Saxberg holds a BA in mathematics and a BS in electrical engineering from the University of Washington. As a Rhodes scholar, he received an MA in mathematics from Oxford University. He also received a PhD in electrical engineering and computer science from MIT and an MD from Harvard Medical School.

Visit http://www.kaplan.com/brorsblog to find out more about learning engineering work at Kaplan.

Dedications

Rick

For my dad, who taught me everything I know about technology, and for my nephew Eli, who finds desktop computers as anachronistic as slide rulers.

Bror

For my mother and father, who supported and challenged my brother and me—they barely survived!—and for Denise, Haakon, Siri, and Tor, whose patience and love always fuel my thinking.

CHAPTER 1

Introduction

You can hardly open a newspaper, visit an education website, or peruse cable news without encountering enthusiastic accounts of new education technologies. Advocates excitedly tout online courses, computer-adaptive assessments, iPad adoption, Khan Academy, virtual schools, hybrid schools, and a wealth of Silicon Valley-ish education technology startups with clever names.

We often hear promises that digital learning will improve schools, enrich learning, and empower educators and students. Yet technology can't and won't make these things happen by itself.

After all, while educational technology *always* seems to be ripe with promise, experiences using new technologies in classrooms over the course of the past century or so have left educators exasperated and wary. Decade after decade, disappointing initiatives have soaked up time, energy, and money while showing little evidence that new tools actually deliver on their promise to make a difference for learners.

We say this not because we doubt technology's potential, but because its realization requires a degree of seriousness, humility, and skepticism that has too often been lacking. To our minds, the disappointing legacy of educational technology has been less about the technology than about how we've used it. The success of this digital moment in schools will ultimately hinge on this human element—how educators and educational leaders approach, apply, and adopt new technologies. That's where this book comes in.

THINKING LIKE A LEARNING ENGINEER

Engineers are the world's most creative and effective problem solvers. That's because they combine imaginative thinking with an appreciation for how the world really works. Engineers in any field operate by identifying problems to be solved, designing smart solutions consistent with the relevant science, and figuring out how to make those solutions feasible. It's our contention that education has suffered for its dearth of engineers. In fact, we think, this is why so many of our debates seem to go nowhere. Engineers can bring fresh, workable approaches to stubborn problems. As Donald Coduto, civil engineer and professor at California State Polytechnic University, Pomona, once wrote, "Some say the cup is half empty, while others say it is half full. However, in my opinion both are wrong. The real problem is the cup is too big. Sometimes all we need is a new perspective on an old problem."[1]

When it comes to realizing the promise of digital technology, educators need to start approaching these challenges as *learning engineers*. While such a label may sound unfamiliar at first, stick with us for a moment. Learning engineering is what tech-savvy educational leaders—and more than a few who aren't so tech-savvy—already do every day (whether they know it or not). These educators ask what problems need to be solved for students, turn to research to identify solutions, and devise smarter, better ways to promote terrific teaching and learning. What is education technology's role in all of this? Learning engineers see this technology *as a tool, not a solution.*

In fact, just about everything in a school, classroom, or learning environment should be regarded this way. And we mean *everything.* For example, a team at Kaplan, Inc., an education provider that serves more than a million students a year, was frustrated that classroom furniture was compromising teaching and learning.[2] While classroom furniture isn't usually regarded as an education technology, it should be. Tables and chairs are tools for learning, just like books, pencils, whiteboards, and laptops. In fact, a 2013 study from England's University of Salford found that classroom architecture and design factors like classroom orientation, natural light, noise, and use of space had a measurable impact on student learning.[3]

Kaplan classroom furniture

Yet traditional classroom desks and chairs often make it tough for students to collaborate or rotate through activities without wasting time and disrupting instructional flow. In response, Kaplan started piloting new furniture designs from Steelcase, an office furniture company. The new chairs and tables can be easily reconfigured from a lecture-style class setting, to paired or group arrangements, and back again. Kaplan is now collecting data to see how the new configurations are actually working and what modifications are

Kaplan classroom furniture

needed. This is learning engineering, applied to furniture.

We'd be surprised if Ford, General Electric, or Apple adopted new technological products without carefully scrutinizing what works, what doesn't, what's annoying, and why. Think about how rapidly Internet firms like Amazon or Facebook modify their offerings in response to complaints and feedback. Indeed, designers take care to consider what science and research can teach them about energy use, aerodynamic efficiency, convenience, and the rest—and then they try it out, see what happens, try to rapidly fix mistakes, and keep going.

At their best, engineers apply "design thinking"—systematic efforts to deeply understand practical problems, generate possible solutions, and then winnow those down to things that can work in practice.[4] If you start by diagnosing the problems your users are having, and focus on what's actually possible, it's amazing what kinds of solutions can be engineered.[5]

In schooling, that same discipline has too often been lacking. In a 2013 report from the Center for American Progress, a liberal think tank in Washington, DC, senior fellow Ulrich Boser concluded, "Schools frequently acquire digital devices without discrete learning goals and ultimately use these devices in ways that fail to adequately serve students, schools, or taxpayers."[6] We're confident that educators can do a lot better, and that doing so is a matter of will and of skill.

WHY THIS VOLUME?

Why this book? After all, there already are a number of terrific books on education technology. Several years ago, Harvard Business School professor Clay Christensen, along with Michael Horn and Curtis Johnson, sparked interest in digital learning with the popular *Disrupting Class.*[7] The authors argued that technology, and the promise of mass customization, has the potential to upend traditional notions of how schooling should be delivered. Christensen and Horn proceeded to found the California-based Innosight Institute in 2007 (renamed the Clayton Christensen Institute for Disruptive Innovation in 2013), which has since championed tech-enabled educational innovation and produced influential work on "blended" learning.[8]

Other authors have observed that technology can help reimagine outdated schools and systems. A few years ago, Stanford University's Terry Moe and National Association of Independent Schools President John Chubb argued in *Liberating Learning: Technology, Politics, and the Future of American Education,* "The great promise of technology for American education . . . is not that it makes the schools perfect or trouble free. Its great promise is that it stands to make them significantly *better* over time by transforming the underlying fundamentals of the system."[9] Harvard University professor Paul Peterson struck similar notes regarding the transformative power of technology in the final chapter of his sweeping historical narrative *Saving Schools: From Horace Mann to Virtual Learning.*[10]

Still others have explained how technology can change teaching, learning, and school design. In his book *Getting Smart: How Digital Learning Is Changing the World,* Tom Vander Ark, a partner at LearnCapital, argues that digital learning will generate vast new data on learning and student performance.[11] Harvard University professor Chris Dede's *Digital Teaching Platforms* features a slew of experts examining how new tools make it possible to customize learning.[12] And in *Brain Gain: Technology and the Quest for Digital Wisdom,* author and speaker Marc Prensky argues that technology enlivens learning and enhances cognition.[13]

Readers may also be familiar with texts that provide technology-specific guidance for school and system leaders; such volumes include former teacher and technology specialist Susan Brooks-Young's *Critical Technology Issues for School Leaders,* City University of New York professor Anthony Picciano's *Educational Leadership and Planning for Technology,* and celebrated Mooresville Graded School District Superintendent Mark Edwards's *Every Child, Every Day.*[14] In his lively account, Edwards recounts his North Carolina district's five-year journey through a "digital conversion" to national acclaim (we'll hear more about Mooresville later).

Each of these works is valuable and worth perusing. But what we offer here, which we think is distinctive and important, is a guide to help school and system leaders understand more about how learning works and how that knowledge can inform their approach to technology. To be clear, we're also firmly convinced that these same habits of mind can help inform smart school redesign with *or without* technology.

At this point, we'd be remiss if we failed to mention Larry Cuban's terrific 2002 volume, *Oversold and Underused: Computers in the Classroom.*[15] We think those who suggest that technology is inexorably changing the face of American schooling would do well to revisit Cuban's book. He reminds us that such claims have been made before (many times!) and have as often disappointed when highly touted new technologies were misused, marginalized, or used to little effect. Of this frustrating history, Cuban observes, "Although promoters of new technologies often spout the rhetoric of fundamental change, few have pursued deep and comprehensive changes in the existing system of schooling."[16]

We do not believe that such a fate is inevitable. Indeed, we see enormous potential for using new tools to rethink and redesign teaching, learning, and schooling. But that will not happen of its own accord. Indeed, the outcome will hinge more on the rethinking and redesigning than on the technology. Yet, that rethinking and redesigning is where we have persistently come up short. We hope to help education leaders do something about that.

THE BOOK: THE WORLD'S MOST SUCCESSFUL EDUCATION TECHNOLOGY

The history of education technology is rife with disappointment (we'll have more to say on this shortly). But we firmly believe that technology can have a catalytic impact on learning. We're confident of this, in part, because it's happened before. In fact, we can think of at least one technology that irrevocably and universally transformed teaching and learning. Originally greeted by educators with skepticism and suspicion, it has gone on to help redefine the very fabric of schooling.

What do we have in mind? Your familiar, friendly book. Indeed, it's now so familiar that it's hard to imagine that it hasn't always been with us. But it hasn't. Heck, *writing* hasn't always been with us. In *A History of Writing*, author Steven Roger Fischer aptly describes writing as "human knowledge's ultimate tool."[17] And, like every new tool, writing had its detractors. Socrates was a big skeptic, having come of age in an era when learning was a matter of oral instruction and memorization. He feared that once stories could be written down, they would no longer need to be memorized, which would undermine mental discipline.[18]

Parchment, made from stretched and dried animal skin, first emerged in the second century BC. In the centuries that followed, manuscripts were handwritten and reproduced by scribes. This put ideas and information into a durable form that could be viewed repeatedly, but writing on parchment was a laborious process that made it a feat to produce even a handful of copies. Scribes could work only during daylight hours, as working by candle or lantern posed too great a risk of fire.[19] Hired scribes would take weeks, months, or even years to copy a document by hand. The result: Printed material spread at a painstaking pace, and books were rare and prized possessions.

The book, as we know it today, first became available in the 15th century with the invention of the printing press. Fischer explains in *A History of Writing*, "Printing changed society in a fundamental way. By making almost unlimited copies of identical texts available by mechanical (now electronic) means, it brought society from limited access to knowledge to almost unlimited access to knowledge."[20] Statistician Nate Silver has noted, "Almost overnight, the cost of producing a book decreased by about three hundred times, so a book that might have cost $20,000 in today's dollars instead cost $70."[21] That change led to an explosion in the availability of books.

At the time, the printing press was hardly seen as an unmitigated blessing. Religious educators feared that willy-nilly access to printed material would threaten the church's ability to ensure that important truths were learned in the correct, approved fashion. They worried that students and parishioners might learn the "wrong" stuff if left to their own devices, absent a teacher's moral and interpretive guidance.

There were also fears that mass printed books were a poor, cheap substitute for the rich (if restricted) experience of reading a scribe-written parchment. In 1492, abbot Johannes Trithemius bemoaned the printing press, opining, "Among all the manual exercises, none is so seemly to monks as devotion to the writing of sacred texts. . . . Printed books will never equal scribed books, especially because the spelling and ornamentation of some printed books is often neglected. Copying requires greater diligence. . . . Scripture on parchment can persist a thousand years, but on paper, how long will it last? It's a great thing if a paper volume lasts two hundred years."[22]

What to make of all this? Can it really inform our thinking about 21st century education technology? Well, yes. Especially if we note that books did two things in particular. First, they allowed students to learn from any expert in the world (who chose to put his thoughts on paper) and meant students were no longer restricted to the knowledge of village authorities. Second, they unshackled learning from the confines of the teacher-led classroom. Now, students could take a book home, read it there, and come to school prepared to discuss what they'd read outside of class.

The book ultimately made it possible to rethink the classroom and the role of the teacher. Books revolutionized the provision of information, letting students read and reread text as often as they needed. This made it easier to grasp and apply new ideas. Before books, teachers had been primarily responsible for telling stuff to students—for lecturing. Any student or class could learn only as much as the teacher could convey. The book made high-quality content readily available to anyone with a copy, at any time, day or night. No longer dependent on what one teacher knew, a student could read a "lecture" penned by the foremost authority on a given question.

This allowed students to master content by perusing their books, freeing the teacher to focus on tasks besides just conveying knowledge—to do more explaining or mentoring. You see where this is going—*books* provided the first opportunity to "flip" a classroom, an in-vogue term which means students pick up information outside of school. The term's current use implies non-print media, but books were also intended to "flip" the classroom through reading, allowing students to absorb new material even when a teacher wasn't lecturing.

Today, centuries after the invention of the printing press, it's hard to imagine schooling without the book. Watch a typical classroom and one sees that the shape of a teacher's job is wrapped around the textbook. Teachers expect students to read textbook chapters at home, allowing classroom instruction to emphasize understanding and exploration. Teachers ask high schoolers to read novels, so that they can discuss them in class. Until very recently, when such activities started to migrate online, students were referred to books for additional explanation or when pursuing research. This allowed teachers, at least in theory, to focus more of their in-class energy on explaining, mentoring, coaching, and all the rest, and to reduce time spent providing facts or reciting content.

In short, books did some of the same things that we excitedly seek from online learning today—it's just that books did them in a much more limited, less agile, and less customizable fashion.

BOOKS *ARE* A LEARNING TECHNOLOGY

Let's make sure we're perfectly clear: Books *are* a learning technology, even without electricity or an on-off switch. And, like all technologies, they can be used in ways that are more or less likely to improve teaching and learning.

Famed psychologist and educator Benjamin Bloom pointed out years ago that, while we've been trying to improve textbooks for a very long time, most of the fiddling hadn't obviously affected student learning. The only exception, he noted, was where teachers were carefully trained in using the new text or curriculum.[23] In other words: It's not the book, it's what you do with it. As with any other technology, books can be made, and used, well . . . or poorly.

The benefits of the book are readily apparent. Books make information widely available. They permit students to move at their own pace and to read and reread passages as needed, providing the opportunity for repetition and reinforcement that is (as we will see in Chapter 2) so essential for mastering knowledge. Books make it possible for students to learn during the summer, in the evening, and even when they're ill or assigned to an inept teacher.

In the terminology of Harvard Business School's Clay Christensen, books truly were a "disruptive technology." They radically transformed the economics and possibilities of learning, making a stripped-down education available to those who had previously been denied even a semblance of schooling. Books took something that already existed—lectures and stories—and made them more affordable, available, and reliable. For the vast majority of students, books are a huge improvement over the alternative—lectures delivered by instructors of uneven knowledge, availability, and skill.

But books also have real limitations. They are fundamentally visual—they are unable to tap into our second major channel for learning, the auditory system. They are also profoundly nonadaptive. By design, books have to be pitched at some median reader—the phrasing, flow, structure, and presentation of a given book are fixed. If the material and language are too difficult for one reader or not challenging enough for another, so be it. Thus, when teaching reading, for instance, we tend to offer a series of books, allowing us to match levels to the reader in question. Note, though, that the books themselves are still static; a series of readers is just a way to work around that limitation.

Indeed, for the fortunate handful of students able to sit in a classroom with eminent thinkers, reading a book may well have been inferior to absorbing a lesson delivered by a phenomenal teacher or hearing a story told by a gifted narrator. However, for many students, the alternative to a book was no education at all. Books aren't "good" or "bad": they are just one potentially powerful tool for teaching and learning. We've all witnessed classrooms where students sat stolidly hour after hour, hunched over tedious textbooks. We've all seen students struggle with poorly written, boring texts. We've all seen teachers whose idea of a spiral lesson was to repeat the sections of the textbook, occasionally interspersed with questions from the teacher's edition. We've all seen an unfortunate class spend a period taking turns reading textbook passages aloud. The key is not the book, but how wisely and well it's used. That's where learning engineering comes in.

A DISPIRITING TRACK RECORD

Books created vast opportunities to expand and enrich learning, and to rethink teaching. They were also limited, with their value depending on how they were used. The same is true of more modern technologies. You'd think that with all the new technology that's emerged in recent decades, we'd have seen quantum leaps in learning. We haven't. Why? We suspect it's because we've hardly ever replicated what the book got right. We haven't used education technologies to rethink teaching and learning, change the job description of teachers, or really upend assumptions about when, where, and how learning should happen.

Instead, seduced by ed-tech proselytizers, it's easy for enthusiastic policymakers, would-be reformers, and system leaders to imagine that all they need to do is stir some technology into schools and classrooms and wait for the magic to happen. Schools and systems then wind up adopting any number of potentially promising ideas—from online instruction to one-to-one devices to hybrid school models—without understanding what it will take for the technology to really transform teaching and learning.

There are plenty of disheartening examples from the past. Readers of a certain age may remember those bulky classroom filmstrips about wildlife, or mind-numbing films explaining scientific experiments (with scenes that looked as if they could be canned footage from television's *Lost*). It's easy to forget how much confidence there once was that these inventions could revolutionize learning. After all, schools first used films in 1910. By 1931, 25 states had departments dedicated to educational film and related media.[24] In 1922, Thomas Edison proclaimed that "the motion picture is destined to revolutionize our educational system. . . . In a few years it will supplant largely, if not entirely, the use of textbooks."[25] The way it turned out: not so much.

The story of radio was similar. In 1923, New York City's Haaren High School was the first to use the radio for classroom instruction, broadcasting a lecture to an accounting class.[26] In 1931, Commissioner of Education William J. Cooper established a radio section in the U.S. Office of Education.[27] By 1932, nine states broadcast weekly and monthly educational programs. That year, Benjamin Darrow, author of *Radio: The Assistant Teacher,* termed radio a "vibrant and challenging textbook of the air," saying it could "become a tremendous agency for public school education."[28] By the 1940s, more than half of schools had radio equipment. In 1945, William Levenson, director of the Cleveland public schools' radio station, said "a portable radio receiver will be as common in the classroom as is the blackboard."[29] Yet, for all that, principals said radios were underutilized in practice, due to a lack of resources, scheduling difficulties, and programs that weren't tied to the curriculum.[30] (Sound familiar?) Today, the notion that radio was ever going to be a powerful learning tool seems quaint, if not silly.

Television was once heralded as the next frontier for schools and classrooms. In the 1960s, the Ford Foundation invested $20 million in the use of television in 250 school systems, and President John F. Kennedy secured a $32 million congressional appropriation for developing classroom television.[31] By 1971, over $100 million in public and private funds had been spent on educational television.[32] Once again, surveys showed that teachers weren't using the televisions. Larry Cuban notes, "Students spent more time going and coming from the bathroom than watching televised lessons."[33] For the few teachers who did use TV, there was little serious preparation, deliberate follow-up, or lesson integration.[34] (Again, sound familiar?)

More recently, in the 1980s and 1990s, desktop computers sparked grand hopes. Those didn't pan out either. In *Oversold and Underused: Computers in the Classroom,* Larry Cuban observed, "In the schools we studied, we found no clear and substantial evidence of students increasing their academic achievement as a result of using information technologies."[35] Instead, "The overwhelming majority of teachers employed the technology to sustain existing patterns of teaching rather than to innovate."[36] Same story, different decade.

Handheld devices, laptops, tablets, and smartboards are the new darlings of the smart set. More than a decade ago, back in 2000, at the height of the millennial tech boom, Maine Governor Angus King made a splash by giving laptops to each of the state's seventh graders. He said his goal was to "do something different from what everybody else is doing."[37] The only thing missing from the $50 million proposal was any clear notion of how this would enhance learning, alter the role of teachers, or do anything of particular value. This is a common tale. As part of the international One Laptop per Child Initiative, the nation of Peru spent $200 million to distribute laptops to 800,000 students. A 2012 study found no evidence of improved learning.[38]

Examples of ineffective technology utilization abound. A painfully typical case was the Virginia Department of Education's "Beyond Textbooks" initiative. In September 2010, Virginia used a $150,000 grant to buy 350 iPads, giving them to four districts with hardly any attention to how they would be used. The state superintendent explained, "The experiences of students and teachers will be evaluated, and the knowledge gained will help policy makers, educators and our private sector partners better understand the potential instructional uses of interactive digital media and wireless technology."[39] After 18 months, an evaluation concluded that students "liked the e-book's ability to support individualized learning" and "felt comfortable reading and using an e-book."[40] OK, then.

By 2012, Apple reported that it had sold over 1.5 million iPads to U.S. education institutions, with over 1,000 locales featuring one-to-one adoptions.[41] As of that year, K–12 school systems made up 60 percent of the 100 biggest publicly-known iPad deployments.[42] In fall 2012, there were over 70,000 education-related apps in the iTunes store alone.[43] Talking to these schools and systems yields little confidence that things will work better than in the past. Anthony Kim, CEO of Education Elements, which helps school systems integrate technology, finds districts more focused on buying gadgets than on using them. He says, "We see districts buy 1,000 iPads and deploy them out to the schools. They get all excited and the parents get excited. But the schools don't know what to do with them." In short, they've missed the chance to do the learning engineering that could make a difference.

For all these successive waves of technology and "innovation," the rhythms, routines, and regularities of American schools and classrooms have remained remarkably static. Adding insult to injury, a 2007 congressionally mandated study by the National Center for Education Evaluation examined education technology in 33 school districts, and found no evidence that tech-enabled classrooms have helped boost student achievement.[44]

Back in 1996, in *The End of Education,* mass media critic Neil Postman scathingly charged, "We must be more modest about this god of Technology and certainly not pin our hopes on it. . . . After all, it is an old quest. As early as 1918, H.L. Mencken (although completely devoid of empathy) wrote, 'There is no sure-cure so idiotic that some superintendent of schools will not swallow it. The aim seems to be . . . to discover some master formula that will not only take the place of competence and resourcefulness in the teacher but that will also create an artificial receptivity in the child.'"[45]

Postman continued, "Mencken was not necessarily speaking of technological panaceas, but he may well have been." Postman quotes a poem, penned by a teacher in the early 1920s:

> Mr. Edison says
>
> That the radio will supplant the teacher.
>
> Already one may learn languages by means of Victrola records.
>
> The moving picture will visualize
>
> What the radio fails to get across.
>
> Teachers will be relegated to the backwoods . . .[46]

Postman mused, "I do not go back as far as the introduction of the radio and the Victrola, but I am old enough to remember when 16-millimeter film was to be the sure-cure, then closed-circuit television, then 8-millimeter film, then teacher-proof textbooks. Now computers."[47]

What can school and system leaders do to break the cycle of overpromising and disappointment?

THE "THREAT" OF TECHNOLOGY

While skepticism is well-founded when it comes to big talk regarding education technology, overwrought fears about the perils of technology have proven equally exaggerated. Those apprehensive about computer-assisted tutoring or online instruction would do well to keep in mind that such concerns have greeted almost any new learning tool. Dave Thornburg and David Dwyer, for instance, offer up a list of past complaints in their book *Rethinking Education in the Age of Technology: The Digital Revolution and Schooling in America*. From today's vantage point, some of the concerns make for amusing reading:

> From a principal's publication, 1815: "Students today depend on paper too much. They don't know how to write on a slate without getting chalk dust all over themselves. They can't clean a slate properly. What will they do when they run out of paper?"

From the journal of the National Association of Teachers, 1907: "Students today depend too much upon ink. They don't know how to use a pen knife to sharpen a pencil. Pen and ink will never replace the pencil."

From *Federal Teachers,* 1950: "Ballpoint pens will be the ruin of education in our country. Students use these devices and then throw them away. The American values of thrift and frugality are being discarded. Businesses and banks will never allow such expensive luxuries."

A fourth-grade teacher in the 1987 Apple Classroom of Tomorrow chronicles: "If students turn in papers they did on the computer, I require them to write them over in long hand because I don't believe they do the computer work on their own."[48]

A LOT OF POTENTIAL

In November 2012, the cover story of *Forbes* was "One Man, One Computer, 10 Million Students: How Khan Academy Is Reinventing Education."[49] The breathless tone reflected the magical hope that the power of the web, mobile computing, ubiquitous video, and cheap, powerful devices will revolutionize teaching and learning.

Technology truly does offer some breakthrough capabilities, due to steady improvement in computer memory, processing speed, disk space, and user interfaces. Thirty years ago, it was unusual for a family to have a single computer at home. Today, we routinely use smartphones and tablets that each possess more computing power than an expensive desktop computer had a generation ago.

Vast improvements in data bandwidth are remaking whole industries. Landlines are being eclipsed by digital wireless technologies. The music, publishing, and video industries have been fundamentally changed by the ability to nimbly move around massive digital files, instantly providing high-quality experiences to billions of users.

The accessibility of information online means we now expect complex queries to be rapidly answered from anywhere. It's not just data that we expect to move fast. Today's technologies mean that we can fly from Seattle to Stockholm in a matter of hours with as little as a day's notice. These shifts have transformed national economies and allowed work to be "outsourced" in ways that were once unimaginable (as when paralegals in New Delhi comb through depositions from a bank fraud case playing out in New Brunswick).

It's now possible to connect with whomever, whenever, to form communities and friendships with people who live half the world away. Twenty years ago, mobile phones had frustratingly limited coverage—and most Americans regarded the ungainly devices as a needless extravagance. Now, whole swaths of the world reflexively use smartphones to access social media in order to keep up with the news and stay current with what friends and colleagues are doing.

In short, technology has materially transformed key aspects of our daily lives, changing what we can do and how we do it, and speeding up knowledge sharing, communication, and activity while saving money and time. We think it's perfectly appropriate to expect the same thing in schooling.

MYTHS THAT SUFFUSE AND CONFUSE RETHINKING

The path to such improvement begins with puncturing several popular myths that have promised an easy path, suggested the rigors of learning engineering are unnecessary, and bred an undue faith in the inexorability of K–12's "digital revolution":

Today's kids are different because they are digital natives. It's true that kids grow up around computers, smartphones, and the rest, and that many may be more comfortable online than in their backyard. But this tells us nothing about how to respond to the challenge of leveraging technology to rethink schooling. If we're trying to figure out how to help students master knowledge, practice skills, or become better readers, it's not clear that being a "digital native" has any special import. This reassuring mantra can be an excuse to avoid the hard work of figuring out how to put student interests and skills to good use.

More technology yields more learning. School and system leaders are fond of pointing to all the technological stuff they've acquired, as if more devices equal more learning. Despite all local evidence to the contrary, the technology education director of one large urban school system insisted in 2011, "What we've found with the iPads as we've rolled this out is that having kids with a device such as the iPad in the classroom—within the curriculum— is very powerful."[50] Matt Federoff, chief information officer in Vail, Arizona, wryly notes, "We have enough wireless to make your fillings hurt."[51] Talking to principals or system leaders about technology is often a lot like talking to the mechanic who's fixing your car and having him proudly show you his wrench collection. That's swell and all, but you probably care less about his tools than what he's doing with them. As Richard Clark, director of the Center for Cognitive Technology at the University of Southern California, pointed out back in 1983, more technology matters only if it promotes good teaching and learning.[52] Too often, it doesn't.

Adding technology is anti-teacher. One of the bizarre fault lines in education technology is the notion that people are either "pro-machine" or "pro-teacher." In 2012, the *New York Times* quoted one teacher saying, of her use of the Socratic method, "I'm teaching [students] to think deeply, to think. A computer can't do that."[53] The president of the Idaho Education Association said in 2011, in an article titled "Laptops Are Not Teachers," "You simply cannot replace a teacher with a laptop."[54] Well, OK. But that reaction misses the point. We rarely hear anyone suggest that X-rays or surgical lasers can "replace" doctors or debate whether we're "for" surgical lasers or "for" doctors. We would dismiss such talk as nonsense and instead recognize that surgical lasers are a tool that can help doctors do their job more safely, rapidly, precisely, and effectively. That's how we ought to think about technology in schooling.

Virtual schools are different from brick-and-mortar schools, and that's a problem. Virtual schools are obviously different from traditional brick-and-mortar schools in some ways, but let's not forget that traditional schools also vary enormously from one to another. Of far greater import is the fact that virtual schools offer opportunities to support learning in new ways, in new configurations, and to students who previously lacked access. Alone, or as part of a "hybrid" with brick-and-mortar schools, as in the case of Rocketship Education, the Khan Academy flipped-classroom model, or the School of One (all of which we will encounter in later chapters), virtual schooling simply expands the range of ways to support teaching and learning.

There's "not enough" technology to drive transformation. There's an oft-repeated notion that the real key to "change everything" is to get "enough" technology into schools, or that once we get to one-to-one computing, "everything will be different." As we mentioned before, we've seen remarkably little evidence for this. Learning will benefit if, and only if, educators are reengineering their practices, assumptions, routines, and expectations to take full advantage of the new tools at their disposal. One-to-one has generally disappointed because educators have tended to keep doing what they've always done—just with more advanced technology.

The next ***generation of technology will make things different.*** Even among those who readily concede the disappointing track record of ed-tech, there's a constant tendency to attribute it to the fact that previous technology was too frail—but the coming wave will make all the difference. The problem is that improvements in technology turn out to be far less important than how we use them—and a failure to think like learning engineers means that each new "this time it's different" advance ultimately winds up disappointing. As Will Richardson, former teacher and author of *Blogs, Wikis, Podcasts, and Other Powerful Web Tools for Classrooms,* writes, "When I hear school leaders talk about spending thousands of dollars on devices to make students more engaged or to 'personalize' instruction, I know they mean to change little, if anything, of what learning looks like in classrooms. Old wine, new bottles. . . . Right now we should be asking ourselves not just how to do school better, but how to do it decidedly differently."[55]

Bottom line: Take a look in the mirror. It's not the technology, people. It's us, and what we do with it.

CARPE DIEM: REENGINEERING WHAT IT MEANS TO BE A "SCHOOL"

What does it look like to operate like a learning engineer? Consider Carpe Diem Collegiate High School and Middle School in Yuma, Arizona. Founded in 2002 by Rick Ogston, former president of the

Arizona Charter School Association, Carpe Diem featured a "blended" learning model, combining computer-assisted instruction with redesigned classrooms. Carpe Diem offers a radical twist on the familiar schoolhouse: More than 200 personal cubicles, each containing a computer, fill the single room that makes up one floor of the school. *Hechinger Report*

A view inside Carpe Diem

journalist Nick Pandolfo has noted that it "looks more like an office or call center than a school."[56] Students split their time between individualized online instruction on their personal computers and teacher-led collaborative workshops.

At the heart of the redesign was a desire to help students learn better. As Ogston explains, "Now, the chalkboard model may seem more 'efficient,' since you have a lot of people doing the same thing at the same time, but it's not very good for learning. I was looking to see how we could provide more individualized and personalized instruction for kids. And, at this point in time, the best way to do that is to leverage technology. Now if you can find a better way, great."

The key, Ogston says, is to understand technology as a tool rather than an answer. He says, "When you're leveraging technology like we are, people want to look at us in terms of technology. But the secret sauce is not the technology, it's the relationships. The downstairs is the collaborative social learning environment, and the upstairs looks like a call center. People say this looks impersonal. I say, 'Well, as opposed to a classroom with rows of desks and a teacher lecturing?' You know, that doesn't strike me as real personal, either. The upstairs offers space that's separate and non-social so that students can focus on their own path and the downstairs is a place for collaboration. That's the blend that we find works."

Ogston notes that the Carpe Diem design required "the entire ecosystem to change, including the role of teacher, parent, student, and administrator." The school has five teachers and four teacher

Carpe Diem students at work

aides for 226 students, with each teacher teaching all the students in their subject, regardless of grade level.

So, for instance, Carpe Diem has one math teacher for all students in grades 6–12. It's not about economy, Ogston explains, but about cultivating relationships that can span across grade levels and reduce the learning curve required for teachers and students to start from scratch each year. Ogston says that teachers get to know their students, their career goals, their family, and their learning needs.

Ogston came to education not as a career educator but after earlier stints in the Marines, in business, as a family therapist, and as a church pastor. When he entered schooling, he eventually earned an MEd and found himself running two charter schools. In that role, Ogston recalls, "Just like I had feared, I realized one day that we had re-created the traditional system." Ogston's eclectic background may have helped equip him to think differently about technology and school design. Nearly a decade ago, he sat down with a consultant and a computer to explore what was possible. He remembers, "I didn't know the terms and all the pedagogy. . . . I ended up creating the model just by asking questions. Then I put that on the shelf. A year and a half later, the building we were leasing was being sold out from under us and we needed a new home. With this new model, I didn't need all these individual classrooms, I just needed one large space—a call center would be fine. We found a space and did a conversion in three months."

Carpe Diem has delivered some promising results, while serving a student population that was 46 percent free and reduced lunch students in 2011–12: Carpe Diem ranks among Arizona's 10 highest-performing charter schools, outperforming Arizona's statewide four-year graduation rate five of the six years between 2007 and 2012 (with a 96 percent graduation rate in 2011), and regularly exceeding the Arizona average at every grade level on the statewide assessment.[57]

The Carpe Diem model is also cost-effective. It requires fewer teachers per student than a traditional school, so Carpe Diem has achieved those results with only about $5,300 of its $6,300 per pupil allocation, according to Ryan Hackman, the school's chief operating officer.[58] Most of the balance goes toward paying off the bond on the $2.6 million facility or to procuring technology (the school sets aside 2.5 percent of its budget, or about $50,000 a year, for this purpose).[59] Ogston says of the model, "One of the wonderful benefits of what we do is that it becomes more economical, even though it wasn't designed with that in mind. Now, teachers unions are making accusations that computers will replace the teachers. My usual retort is, 'If a computer can replace you, then it probably should.' They tend to just gasp and stare at me. And I go on to explain that a really good teacher could never be replaced by a computer. And so, if you think you could be, then, maybe you should evaluate what kind of a teacher you are."

Ogston notes there are plenty of stumbling blocks and pitfalls for learning engineers. He wryly acknowledges, "I've been stupid. When I started this, I didn't know anything. And I didn't know what I didn't know." And, he says, "I think we're still like 10 years behind where we should be. But technology and financial limitations tend to impinge upon my happy exploration."

For others pursuing tech-enabled redesign, he advises, "The most important thing is the vision of what it is you're going to do. Do your research on technology. Are you simply trying to overlay technology on top of the existing system? Or is it a transformational initiative to truly personalize education? Once you've got a vision, there are various kinds of support that are needed in terms of curriculum and infrastructure. Trying to backfill technology into existing systems can be difficult."

Radical? We suppose. But what we find most interesting is that in using technology to rethink the schoolhouse, Carpe Diem has focused on the latter, not the former.

DON'T GET STUCK ON BOGEYMEN

We can hear the familiar concerns. "Hold up! What's all this talk of rethinking and cost effectiveness? These are children that we're talking about!" After all, K–12 schooling has long been suspicious of ideas that seem too "businesslike." Indeed, the very term "productivity" can set teeth on edge. As education historian Diane Ravitch has charged, "Some advocates of online instruction say it will make possible reductions of 30 percent of today's teaching staff. . . . The bottom line is profits, not students."[60]

We see things a little differently. We'd remind readers that making "productive" use of teachers, time, and money is nothing more than ensuring that schools are promoting great teaching and learning to the best of their ability. Whether efficiencies are seen as a chance to provide more learning time, technology, instruction, or anything else is a determination we think will inevitably (and reasonably) be made by educators, parents, and public officials.

Skepticism about "productivity" is sometimes coupled with doubts that technology can help much. As the late Senator Daniel Patrick Moynihan remarked, producing a Mozart quartet two centuries ago required four musicians, four stringed instruments, and, say, 35 minutes. Producing the same Mozart quartet today, he said, requires the same resources. Moynihan's analogy, while correct, is ultimately misleading when applied to schooling. In the arts, what has changed over two centuries is that radio, CDs, television, and digital media have dramatically increased the number of people able to *hear and appreciate* a given performance at an ever-decreasing cost. As with the book, new technology has made available to the general public a pretty fair stand-in for what was once the preserve of the elite. Maybe listening to a digital recording of the Boston Pops over a top-shelf sound system isn't at the same level as seeing them in person in your white tails, but it's a whole lot more accessible and affordable, and it offers a passable version of the experience to millions who would have otherwise never been able to experience the original.

Frankly, that's a big part of technology's promise. If pop stars could only play for a hundred club-goers at a time, they'd be hard-pressed to reach 50,000 listeners a year, even if they played all 365 nights. However, playing to stadiums with digitally amplified sounds and visuals, that same singer can thrill 50,000 in a night. Playing stadiums and sharing songs via online downloads make cheaply available to billions what used to be the province of a fortunate few. Is hearing Lady Gaga in a stadium as "good" an experience as hearing her play a club? Probably not. But, as with the book, it offers the experience to those who otherwise wouldn't . . . you get the idea. Oh, and if Lady Gaga had to work 40 hours a week waiting tables or writing computer code in order to eat, because playing clubs didn't provide a comfortable wage, she would have a lot less time to practice, craft new routines, or cut songs. In other words, the technology-aided experience allows skilled professionals to earn outsized recognition, influence, and compensation while giving them more time to devote to polishing and sharing their craft. In schooling, new technologies offer the promise of extending the impact of terrific teachers, so that they can coach, tutor, or instruct hundreds with the same energy expended to reach five or 25.

Now, let's not get carried away. Any tool has its limits. And there are clearly things that teachers do that can't be done virtually or with technology. But we need to think much more clearly about just what those are. As Cathy Davidson, author of *Now You See It: How the Brain Science of Attention Will Transform the Way We Live, Work, and Learn,* encourages us to ask, "What is happening in the classroom that could not be duplicated by a computer?" Sounding remarkably like Rick Ogston, she observes, "If the answer is 'nothing,' then there is a problem. In fact, I believe that if teachers can be replaced by computers, they should be. By that I mean if a teacher offers nothing that [a] child can't get from a computer screen, then your child might as well be learning online. On the other hand, no screen will ever replace a creative, engaged, interactive, relevant, and inspiring teacher, especially one who takes advantage of the precious face-to-face experience of people learning together."[61] That's the right mind-set. We should not be "pro-technology" or "anti-technology." Rather, we should ask how technology might enhance, expand, or improve learning, and what that will require. That's learning engineering.

LEARNING SCIENCE AND LEARNING ENGINEERS

What we're talking about is not revolutionary. It's really nothing more than educators using learning science and technology to solve practical challenges. In a nutshell, that's what engineers do.

Sure, the familiar caricature of engineers is that they love differential equations and aren't much fun at parties. The reality is different (well, we make no claims about the parties). Engineers solve real-world problems. Lots of them. Repeatedly and creatively.

They do this by taking scientific knowledge, applying it to the problem (whether that involves the strength of steel or the speed of computers), and designing the smartest solution they can find within financial and practical constraints. The best engineers seek optimal solutions that are easy to use well, serve user needs, and directly and practically solve the problem at hand. Think of those folks at Apple who cooked up the iPod, the iPhone, and the iPad—if they were immersed in learning instead of semiconductor device science and consumer device usability. They're what we've got in mind.

Unlike scientists, engineers have to account for real world complications. Ken Koedinger, codirector of the Pittsburgh Science of Learning Center, says of the difference between a scientist and an engineer, "Let me use physics and mechanical engineering as an analogy. Physics comes up with principles. But when engineers have to employ those principles, they have to deal with [practical questions] like the fact that the coefficient of friction depends on the surface that you're using. Engineering is a different game. Good learning design is not just about principles regarding how learning works, but about learning to apply those principles in a particular context."

The Relationship Between Learning Science and Education Practice

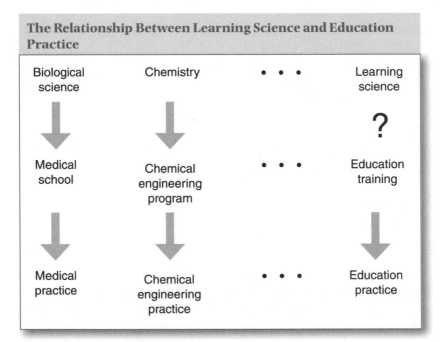

Here's an easier example: Think of physicians as the engineers of biological science. Biologists explore how cells work, organs function, and molecules interact with each other and with bugs, but it's physicians who apply this knowledge to solve health problems for real patients. This includes asking questions like, "How do I keep this medicine refrigerated in the Serengeti?" Physicians know that what works in a lab is still a long way from working "out there" for a patient—and they pilot, train, and monitor accordingly.

The same is true for learning science and learning engineering. We'll talk in more detail about learning science in the next chapter, but, for example, it teaches that learning has to work through our limited, verbal, conscious minds ("working memory") before becoming integrated into our rapid, parallel-processing, nonverbal long-term memory. Moreover, we've learned that this is only possible through lots of deliberate practice with targeted feedback. Unfortunately, this science does not reveal how to organize the work of teachers and students to actually accomplish this, so, like any engineer, we have to apply judgment to the application of the science.

Many factors can contribute to learning difficulties, like awful curricula, mediocre instruction, a lack of timely assessment and student feedback, a lack of discipline, or a student's inability to find time outside school to do what's asked. In many of these cases, technology may have a restorative role to play. But technology isn't always helpful. Indeed, sometimes it can be a distraction. Some readers may recall the early era of desktop publishing, when the earliest Macintosh computers allowed users to select fonts as they liked. Some of us (no names!) created documents festooned with fonts of different kinds, drunk on the opportunity to shift with every paragraph, every page, and every topic. Needless to say, that did not help with the clarity or accessibility of the writing.

Similarly, while we can now view a page from a biochemistry textbook on our iPhone, or even write a term paper on one, this does not mean it's wise to do so. The question is not what can be done with technology, but what technology can do to promote learning. When a principal bragged to us that a student had written a term paper on his smartphone, we could only wonder whether the principal would have bragged that the student wrote a term paper without using his smartphone. If not (and we presume the answer is "no"), then the principal was fixated on the technology rather than the learning. And that's a recipe for disappointment.

THE BOOK AHEAD

Leaders can feel as if they are drowning in a rushing river of ed-tech products and services, and wonder how they're supposed to make sense of it all. That's where learning engineering can prove helpful. It can offer solid footing from which to survey that river and focus not on the shiny things rushing by but on what matters. This means starting with learning science.

The book ahead will unfold accordingly. Chapter 2 provides an introduction to the learning science that matters for students and schools—an introduction to what a learning engineer needs to know. Chapter 3 explains how learning science can be used to think more strategically about education technology. Chapter 4 explores how to apply all this in the context of classrooms and teaching. Chapter 5 shows how schools and systems can be rethought once you bring learning science and technology to bear. Chapter 6 considers some of the barriers and problems that confront learning engineers when they seek to put technology to good use. Finally, Chapter 7 tries to bring all of this together and offer some insights for leaders as they take these ideas back into their schools and systems.

Let's get going.

NOTES

1. Coduto, D. P. (2001). *Foundation design: Principles and practices.* Upper Saddle River, NJ: Prentice Hall. p. 581.
2. Unless otherwise noted, quotations and stories in this book are from first-person accounts or interviews by the authors and/or research associate Taryn Hochleitner between November 2011 and April 2013.
3. University of Salford Manchester. (2013). Study proves classroom design really does matter. Retrieved from http://www.salford.ac.uk/home-page/news/2012/study-proves-classroom-design-really-does-matter

4. Brown, T. (2008, June). Design thinking. *Harvard Business Review.* Retrieved from http://www.unusualleading.com/wp-content/uploads/2009/12/HBR-on-Design-Thinking.pdf

5. Walters, H. (2011). "Design thinking" isn't a miracle cure, but here's how it helps. Fast Company, Co. Design. Retrieved from http://www.fastcodesign.com/1663480/design-thinking-isnt-a-miracle-cure-but-heres-how-it-helps

6. Rich, M. (2013, June 13). Study gauges value of technology in schools. *The New York Times.* Retrieved from http://www.nytimes.com/2013/06/14/education/study-gauges-value-of-technology-in-schools.html?_r=0

7. Christensen, C., Horn, M., & Johnson, C. (2008). *Disrupting class.* New York, NY: McGraw-Hill.

8. For further information about the Clayton Christensen Institute, visit http://www.christenseninstitute.org

9. Moe, T., & Chubb, J. (2009). *Liberating learning: Technology, politics, and the future of American education.* San Francisco, CA: Wiley. p. 179.

10. Peterson, P. (2011). *Saving schools: From Horace Mann to virtual learning.* Cambridge, MA: Belknap Press of Harvard University Press.

11. Vander Ark, T. (2011). *Getting smart: How digital learning is changing the world.* San Francisco, CA: Wiley.

12. Dede, C. (Ed.). (2012). *Digital teaching platforms.* New York, NY: Teachers College Press.

13. Prensky, M. (2012). *Brain gain: Technology and the quest for digital wisdom.* New York, NY: Palgrave.

14. Young, S. B. (2006). *Critical technology issues for school leaders.* Thousand Oaks, CA: Corwin; Picciano, A. (2010). *Educational leadership and planning for technology* (5th ed). New York, NY: Pearson; Edwards, M.A. (2014). *Every child, every day: A digital conversion model for student achievement.* New York, NY: Pearson Education Inc.

15. Cuban, L. (2003). *Oversold and underused: Computers in the classroom.* Cambridge, MA: Harvard University Press.

16. Cuban, L. (2003). *Oversold and underused: Computers in the classroom.* Cambridge, MA: Harvard University Press. p. 195

17. Fischer, S.R. (2001). *A history of writing.* Bury St. Edmunds, Suffolk, UK: St. Edmunsbury Press. p. 7.

18. Jahandarie, K. (1999). *Spoken and written discourse: A multi-disciplinary perspective.* Stamford, CT: Ablex.

19. Finkelstein, D., & Alistair McCleery. (2005). *An introduction to book history.* New York, NY: Routledge.

20. Fischer, S. R. (2001). *A history of writing.* Bury St. Edmunds, Suffolk, UK: St. Edmunsbury Press. p. 285.

21. Silver, N. (2012). *The signal and the noise.* New York: Penguin Press. pp. 2–3.

22. Excerpts from Trithemius, J. (1974 version). *In praise of scribes* (R. Behrendt, Trans). K. Arnold (Ed.). Lawrence, KS: Coronado Press.

23. Bloom, B. (1984). The 2 sigma problem: The search for methods of group instruction as effective as one-to-one tutoring. *Educational Researcher, 13*(6) 4–16, 9. Retrieved from http://www.jstor.org

24. Cuban, L. (1986). *Teachers and machines: The classroom use of technology since 1920.* New York, NY: Teachers College Press. p. 12.

25. Cuban, L. (1986). *Teachers and machines: The classroom use of technology since 1920.* New York, NY: Teachers College Press. p. 9.

26. Cuban, L. (1986). *Teachers and machines: The classroom use of technology since 1920.* New York, NY: Teachers College Press. p. 19.

27. Saettler, L. (2004). *The evolution of American educational technology* (2nd ed.). Charlotte, NC: Information Age Publishing, Inc., p. 213.

28. Cuban, L. (1986). *Teachers and machines: The classroom use of technology since 1920.* New York, NY: Teachers College Press. p. 19; Saettler, L. (2004). *The evolution of American educational technology* (2nd ed.). Charlotte, NC: Information Age Publishing, Inc. p. 198.

29. Cuban, L. (1986). *Teachers and machines: The classroom use of technology since 1920.* New York, NY: Teachers College Press. p. 19.

30. Cuban, L. (1986). *Teachers and machines: The classroom use of technology since 1920.* New York, NY: Teachers College Press. p. 25.

31. Cuban, L. (1986). *Teachers and machines: The classroom use of technology since 1920.* New York, NY: Teachers College Press. p. 28.

32. Cuban, L. (1986). *Teachers and machines: The classroom use of technology since 1920.* New York, NY: Teachers College Press. p. 28.

33. Cuban, L. (1986). *Teachers and machines: The classroom use of technology since 1920.* New York, NY: Teachers College Press. p. 39.

34. Cuban, L. (1986). *Teachers and machines: The classroom use of technology since 1920.* New York, NY: Teachers College Press.

35. Cuban, L. (2003). *Oversold and underused: Computers in the classroom.* Cambridge, MA: Harvard University Press. p. 133.

36. Cuban, L. (2003). *Oversold and underused: Computers in the classroom.* Cambridge, MA: Harvard University Press. p. 134.

37. Curtis, D. (2003). A computer for every lap: The Maine Learning Technology Initiative. *Edutopia*. Retrieved from http://www.edutopia .org

38. Horn, M. (2012, August 22). No shock as Peru's one-to-one laptops miss mark. *Forbes*. Retrieved at http://www.forbes.com

39. Virginia Department of Education. (2010, September 29). Students in four school divisions trade textbooks for iPads [Press release] Retrieved from http://www.doe.virginia.gov/news/news_releases/ 2010/sep29.shtml

40. Virginia Department of Education. (2010). *Beyond textbooks: Year one report*. Retrieved from http://www.doe.virginia.gov/support/ technology/technology_initiatives/learning_without_boundaries/ beyond_textbooks/year_one_beyond_textbooks_report.pdf

41. Apple Inc. (2012, January 19). Apple reinvents textbooks with iBooks2 for iPad [Press release]. Retrieved from http://www.apple .com/pr/library/2012/01/19Apple-Reinvents-Textbooks-with -iBooks-2-for-iPad.html

42. Lai, E. (2012, October 16). Chart: Top 100 iPad rollouts by enterprises & schools. *Forbes*. Retrieved at http://www.forbes.com

43. App Store Metrics. (2012, September). Retrieved from http://148apps .biz/app-store-metrics/

44. U.S. Department of Education. (2007). *Effectiveness of reading and mathematics software products: Findings from the first student cohort*. Washington, DC: Institute of Education Sciences, National Center for Education Evaluation and Regional Assistance. Dynarski, et al. Retrieved from http://ies.ed.gov/ncee/pdf/20074006 .pdf

45. Postman, N. (1996). *The end of education*. New York, NY: Vintage Books. p. 49

46. Postman, N. (1996). *The end of education*. New York, NY: Vintage Books. p. 49

47. Postman, N. (1996). *The end of education*. New York, NY: Vintage Books. p. 49

48. Collins, A., & Halverson, R. (2009). *Rethinking education in the age of technology: The digital revolution and schooling in America*. New York, NY: Teachers College Press. pp. 30–31.

49. Noer, M. (2012, November 2). One man, one computer, 10 million students: How Khan Academy is reinventing education. *Forbes*. Retrieved from http://www.forbes.com

50. Mulholland, J. (2011, March 29). iPads in the classroom. *Government technology: Solutions for state and local government.* Retrieved from http://www.govtech.com/education/iPads-In-The -Classroom.html

51. Dillon, S. (2010, February 11). Wi-Fi turns rowdy bus into rolling study hall. *New York Times.* Retrieved from http://www.nytimes.com

52. Clark, R. E. (1983). Reconsidering research on learning from media. *Review of Educational Research, 53*(4), 445–459.

53. Richtel, M. (2012, January 3). Teachers resist high-tech push in Idaho schools. *New York Times.* Retrieved from http://www.nytimes .com

54. Walker. T. (2011, April 1). Laptops are not teachers. [Web log post]. Message posted to http://neatoday.org

55. Richardson, W. (2013, March). Students first, not stuff. *Educational Leadership, 70*(6).

56. Pandolfo, N. (2012, September 24). Education nation: In Arizona desert, a charter school competes. *The Hechinger Report.* Retrieved from http://hechingerreport.org

57. PR Newswire. (2012, May 2). Carpe Diem Meridian campus to open in Indianapolis for 2012–2013 school year [Press release]. Retrieved from http://www.prnewswire.com/news-releases/carpe-diem -meridian-campus-to-open-in-indianapolis-for-2012-2013-school -year-149819765.html

58. Pandolfo, N. (2012, September 24). Education Nation: In Arizona desert, a charter school competes. *The Hechinger Report.* Retrieved from http://hechingerreport.org

59. Pandolfo, N. (2012, September 24). Education Nation: In Arizona desert, a charter school competes. *The Hechinger Report.* Retrieved from http://hechingerreport.org

60. Devaney, L. (2012, March 16). Diane Ravitch outlines ed tech's promise, perils. *eSchool news.* Posted on http://www.eschoolnews .com

61. Davidson, C. (2011, December 15). 7 key questions to ask about ed technology, online learning. [Web log post]. Posted on http://www .washingtonpost.com/blogs/answer-sheet/

CHAPTER 2

What We Can Learn
From Learning Science

Engineers don't hastily jump into building something new just because it sounds cool. They start by drawing on specific evidence-based expertise about materials, design principles, and context. When they don't do this, the results can be disastrous:

> After an earthquake in February 2011, the six-story Canterbury Television building in New Zealand collapsed, killing 115 people. In December 2012, after months of investigation into the tragedy, the New Zealand government released a report finding several deficiencies in the building's design, including poorly designed joints, inadequate steel reinforcement, weak ties between the floor and wall, and smooth surfaces on the precast concrete beams, which should have been roughened. The report concluded that the building's collapse was the result of poor design from an inexperienced engineer.[1]

A sturdy building needs a solid foundation. That's why good building engineers start with architectural plans, the nature of building materials, and Newton's laws. Software engineers start with existing code and state-of-the-art programming knowledge. Things are no different when it comes to learning. Learning engineers start with learning science.

This can be tougher than it sounds. As R. Keith Sawyer, associate professor of education at Washington University, explains in *The Cambridge Handbook of the Learning Sciences*, "Redesigning schools so that they are based on scientific research is a mammoth undertaking. . . . Since the beginning of the modern institution of schools, there has been a debate about whether education is a science or an art. The language of science makes some educators nervous."[2]

That's a problem. Because trying to reengineer learning without being versed in the basics of learning is like trying to improve brain surgery without knowing much about the brain.

COGNITIVE SCIENCE AND ITS LESS USEFUL COUSINS

So, what kind of knowledge does a learning engineer use? There are two major kinds of brain-related sciences. The first type concerns *neuroscience and brain science*, which examine how cells in the brain and parts of the brain work. The more useful type for our purposes here is *cognitive science,* which explores how people behave and make decisions.

We know this can sound like a lot of gobbledygook. One of your coauthors remembers sitting with a CEO of an education publishing house and chatting about research on learning. He said, "Our company is tremendously interested in all this! We're even funding neuroscience research!" Your coauthor cautiously inquired, "Did you say 'neuroscience'? Or 'cognitive science'?" The CEO paused and then asked, "There's a difference?"

He was clearly seeking to invest in science to support learning but unaware that he would make more progress, more quickly, by looking directly at the results derived from how humans actually learn. (Another caution from this: Don't assume successful vendors or trusted "experts" necessarily have this stuff right.)

Neuroscience studies the interactions of neurons—the basic building blocks of the nervous system and how they work together. *Brain science* is one level up the food chain, addressing how the brain's structures communicate and behave. This is fascinating stuff. For example, in neuroscience, there's speculation about how changes in the myelin covering nerve axons might help explain why practice builds fluency.[3] In brain science, researchers can now use new technological tools to compare the fMRI scans of dyslexic brains and normal brains observed while students are reading. They can see that scans look different before treatment but look more similar as dyslexic students work to overcome deficits.[4]

This may all sound cool to those versed in this stuff, but for most of us, it's too far removed from the world of real schooling to be helpful. Now, don't get us wrong—we, too, care about myelination studies in the Alaskan meadow vole brain—but right now, the findings are more academic than practical. This could change. The early decades of DNA research didn't do much for health treatments, even while providing fascinating insights into genetic disorders such as Huntington's disease (a mutation in the HTT gene on chromosome 4). Over time, though, the research advanced to the point where it could inform medical decisions in profound ways.[5]

They may emerge eventually but, at least for now, new, evidence-based interventions stemming from neuroscience or brain science are a ways off for schooling. This means there's no practical reason (beyond curiosity and enthusiasm, of course!) for learning engineers to scour the neuroscience literature. And there's every reason to be skeptical of slick-sounding vendors who hitch their wagon to brain science or neuroscience—their interventions might work, but not because "brain scientists" or "neuroscientists" have shown they work. At least not yet.

Cognitive science is a different story: It has the goods learning engineers need. That's not such a surprise, since cognitive science is concerned with how people decide, learn, and behave. It provides a wide range of experimental results about what improves learning—and what doesn't. It sets up models of how minds work and tests real behavior to evaluate these theories. Back in the 19th century, for example, German psychologist Hermann Ebbinghaus discovered critical relationships between repetition and retention in memory—the more repetitions, the longer the retention.[6] Decades of recent work have shed light on the benefits of things like simplifying work to reduce the complexity, or "cognitive load," for learners. (See Clark and Mayer's book *E-Learning and the Science of Instruction* for an excellent synthesis.[7])

THE COGNITIVE REVOLUTION

Oddly enough, technology itself had a major role in making cognitive science useful for learning. It's an example of how applied fields and research fields benefit from intercommunication, just as in the case of biological science and health care.

Back in the late 19th and early 20th century, psychologists had trouble linking complicated new biological information about brains to human behavior. One prominent approach was "behaviorism," which sought to model the brain as a kind of big black box that you couldn't see inside, which responded to stimuli in certain ways based on certain rules. Psychologists tried to figure out the rules for this big black box by observing learning in animals, and applying what they learned about stimuli and responses to humans. This yielded some limited successes, but it turned out that people didn't behave like pigeons. (Who knew?) The field was stymied for decades.

Computing grew up during the middle of the 20th century. At first, the focus was on hardware, leading to massive improvements in the speed of computing as transistors replaced vacuum tubes. As computers became able to do tens, then hundreds, then thousands of computations per second, users had the challenge of figuring out how to tell the machines what to do. As the number of computing elements skyrocketed, it made no sense to tell each one, by hand, what to do—there had to be a better way.

So, computer scientists and mathematicians began to think of computers as information-processors rather than electrical systems. They started using block diagrams to describe the decisions being made, viewing the data not as electrical signals but as blocks of information.

This development in programming helped break the logjam in cognitive science. Cognitive psychologists realized that you could think about what was inside the black box of the mind and start to ask how it stores and processes information, without necessarily knowing how each "bit" of information tied to the biology.

This insight inspired the "cognitive revolution" that changed how psychologists investigated behavior and learning. They saw they could describe a mind's information-processing blocks in a systematic, testable way even without fully understanding the neural machinery. Cognitive psychologists began creating models and doing experiments, yielding fresh insights into behavior and how to change it.

Research in cognitive science—like that addressing motivation, goal-setting, memory, near- and longer-term learning, and learning media—can inform instruction. This is what we loosely term "learning science."

In our experience, far too few educators are introduced to the work of world-class researchers in cognitive science during their training. We're thinking of researchers like Richard Mayer at the University of California Santa Barbara, John Sweller at the University of New South Wales in Sydney, Anders Ericsson at Florida State University, Richard Clark at the University of Southern California, and Ken Koedinger at Carnegie Mellon University. They and their peers have spent decades doing careful work into how learning actually works. This research doesn't get nearly as much visibility in educator and leadership preparation as it warrants; would-be learning engineers would do well to take a closer look (at chapter's end, we offer a recommended reading list in the "Resources on Learning Science" sidebar that can help readers do just that).

BECOMING AN EXPERT

When it comes to learning, a good place to start is at the end: What is our goal? To our minds, the ultimate goal of learning is becoming expert at a subject or task, whether that's reading, moral philosophy, calculus, or badminton. Cognitive science researchers have long asked how learning produces expertise. Readers may have seen some of this work if they've perused Malcolm Gladwell's best-selling book *Outliers,* which does a nice job of popularizing some of this research, especially that of psychologist Anders Ericsson.[8] Indeed, as Gladwell highlights, research suggests that expert performance tends to require something like 10,000 hours of deliberate practice.

"Deliberate practice" is, well, deliberate. It's not just repeating what you know how to do. It means looking closely at your own performance, comparing it to an ideal performance, looking for the missteps, then training to address those. Think of football players reviewing game tapes, thinking constantly about how to play their position better. If this sounds like real work, why, yes, it is—but it is *doable* work.

Think about people you know who have become experts at what they do. A truly expert car mechanic can often tell what's wrong with your car just by listening to the engine. An expert physician can ask just a few questions and tap a little here and there before ordering additional tests to get the diagnosis. An expert musician seems to effortlessly perform complex music—while conveying complex emotions. The expert golfer, even as he addresses the ball, has already factored in weather, wind, distance to the green, and the club he's swinging in order to judge how and how hard to hit the ball. We could go on, but you get the picture.

There are four things experts have in common:

- When it comes to many decisions and procedures in their domains, **they work quickly**.
- When making routine decisions in their domain, **they rarely make mistakes**—even when the decisions are quite complex.

- When they talk about what they routinely do, **they organize their conscious thinking at a completely different level** than nonexperts.
- **They tackle new challenges in their domain faster and more accurately** than novices by organizing their thinking about concepts and principles differently.

Experts work fast, they get it right, they think at a different level, and they're better than the rest of us at tackling new challenges in their area of expertise. This is just what we want for our students.

So, how do we get there? What's going on behind the scenes of an expert mind? Think about this:

You are a good driver, been driving for years. You set out to drive to place A, and then begin thinking about life, work, family—all the hard problems of your week and day. After a while, you look around, and you realize, "Darn it, I'm accidentally heading to place B, and I'm almost there!" You laugh at yourself, change direction, and without further thought about it, set off to place A again.

Who drove you to place B? *You* were busy thinking about work, life, family—so who was in charge of a ton of metal, moving at 40, 50, 60 mph? Driving is not a basic biological process, like breathing. It's a complex decision-making process, with lots of rules, anticipation, and decisions that you had to learn. Yet your mind can execute all of this without involving the conscious *you*.

When you were first learning to drive, it was very different. As you tried to remember which was the brake and which the accelerator, your conscious mind was intently focused on driving—and (hopefully) not much else. Yet with a lot of practice, it becomes automatic.

This is not just true of "mechanical" tasks like driving. Consider this scenario:

A medical student calls in an infectious disease expert to help diagnose a challenging patient. The expert arrives, flipping quickly through the chart and waving the student off, then opens the door to the patient's room. He exchanges pleasantries with the patient, walks around the bed to shake hands with the patient, turns around, makes the diagnosis, looks at his watch, says, "Yes!" (it is lunchtime, after all), and heads to the door.

The medical student stops the expert and asks, "How did you make the diagnosis?" The expert hesitates, looks at the ceiling, crosses his arms, looks at his shoes—he appears to have no clue how he made his diagnosis, much to the consternation of the student.

And then the expert tries to relate what he did: A quick scan of the chart had given him a sense of the possible ailments. When he opened the door to the patient's room, he'd noticed that certain smells were not present, narrowing the range of possible diagnoses. He could see the patient's eyes tracking him as he moved, so that removed more possibilities. As he got closer, he could see the patient's skin tone, his muscle tone, the color of his eyes, the texture of his hair, etc.—effectively, the doctor was a living diagnostic machine, processing information from almost every sense.

Yet, when initially asked, the doctor appeared to have no idea how he had made the diagnosis!

The expert diagnostician executed a very complex, but very familiar, task without consciously thinking about it. To put what he did into words, the expert had to reconstruct his own experience and walk through his visit to the patient's room. Indeed, it was the first time in a long time he'd consciously thought about his diagnostic process for this kind of patient.

What does all this mean for how we think about learning?

HOW MEMORY WORKS

The driver and the doctor illustrate that learning and expertise proceed along two distinct paths. The first path includes the memory and skills that we're conscious of using, and the second encompasses more deeply held knowledge that has long since passed into nonconscious, implicit fluency.

Cognitive psychologists describe the conscious, verbal, slower parts of our mind as our *working memory*. The faster, nonconscious part is our *long-term memory*. Our minds use both of these, together, to make decisions and to learn.[9] At the crudest level, we can say that experts are people who have processed large chunks of essential mastery into their long-term memory. Ultimately, helping learners become expert is about using limited-yet-flexible working memory to deliberately practice decisions and skills, with copious feedback. This eventually builds long-term memory's competence, which then works in tandem with working memory to make decisions.

Working Memory

Working memory is the conscious part of our minds. It's powerful, flexible, adaptable, and capable of tackling new subjects. Working memory can solve the most complex problems and work its way through new, difficult things. But, like a computer with inadequate storage, working memory can't have very many "windows" open at once if you expect it to run smoothly. Working memory requires focus. If it's working on too many things simultaneously, it becomes ineffective.

The number of windows a mind can handle at once is not fixed. For one thing, minds react to circumstances very differently depending on what they already know (in other words, depending on what's already in long-term memory). Let's go back to the driving example. An experienced driver makes many complex decisions without even thinking about them. Working memory takes all of this for granted. For instance, when a GPS tells you to turn left while driving, there's no need for it to also tell you which way to turn the steering wheel in order to go left.

Contrast this with many people's experience with parallel parking. Even experienced drivers may only rarely need to execute this joyous maneuver, which is really quite different from "normal" driving. When parallel parking, a driver spends half his time going backward, the navigation is about the back wheels more than the front wheels, and figuring out which way the steering wheel should turn is suddenly complicated, because it reverses depending on whether the car is going forward or backward—and the driver is doing both in rapid succession.

So, it's no wonder many experienced drivers go silent as they parallel park and are unable to continue a conversation that they could carry on cheerfully while weaving through city traffic. Suddenly, their working memory is completely flooded with *this* task—they can't hand it off to a fluent module in long-term memory. They have to think through each step—hence the sometimes confused staring at the wheel, going first one way, then the other, trying to figure out (consciously and slowly) which way to turn to get the rear wheels to behave.

Now, if you move to Brooklyn and drive every day, fast parallel parking will rapidly become a critical, oft-practiced life skill. In that environment, it's a safe bet that you'll soon enough become an expert and insouciant parallel parker. The repeated practice (and honking amounts of feedback) will fuel the creation of that long-term memory module.

As the parallel parking example suggests, what is a modest task for a trained mind can seem a wildly confusing sprawl of information to a novice mind. Working memory can process just a few "chunks" at a time, but the size of those "chunks" depends on how many relevant modules are already etched in long-term memory. There's a popular notion that we can consciously keep about seven "chunks" in mind at once, (though that's probably an overstatement—the right number is more like four).[10] Now, the more expertise one builds in long-term memory, the more readily information can be processed, and the more capacity working memory appears to have to accommodate bigger chunks. Think about how an expert racecar driver, debater, or video game player responds to the chaotic circumstances of competition, compared

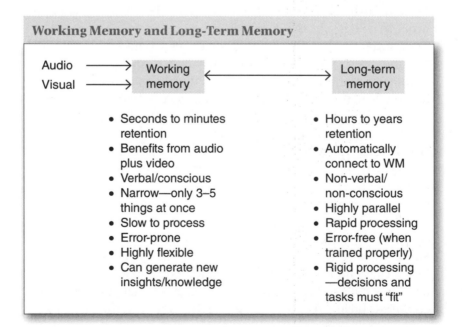

Working Memory and Long-Term Memory

Audio ⟶ Working memory ⟷ Long-term memory
Visual ⟶

Working memory	Long-term memory
• Seconds to minutes retention	• Hours to years retention
• Benefits from audio plus video	• Automatically connect to WM
• Verbal/conscious	• Non-verbal/non-conscious
• Narrow—only 3–5 things at once	• Highly parallel
• Slow to process	• Rapid processing
• Error-prone	• Error-free (when trained properly)
• Highly flexible	• Rigid processing —decisions and tasks must "fit"
• Can generate new insights/knowledge	

to a novice. The novice is overwhelmed with the sights and sounds, but the expert's long-term memory modules pre-process the information down to the critical, manageable chunks that working memory has to focus on.

Long-Term Memory

Put simply, long-term memory is where we store the things that we've mastered. In truth, though, it's much more than that. It's really long-term memory that defines "who we are," given that it determines what we react to immediately, instinctively, naturally, and seemingly without effort. It stores concepts, facts, processes, and principles, but it's also where we store fluent, complex, decision-making procedures like driving or diagnosing a standard illness.

Long-term memory is not conscious; we typically don't even realize what we've stored there, which is why it often gets short shrift in formal education. Working memory has nearly instantaneous access to the complex capabilities stored in long-term memory, making them seem "easy" and "natural" (in sharp contrast to challenges we tackle with working memory alone). When one has so thoroughly learned whole sets of decision making and tasks that they can be done without conscious thought, we call that expertise. That's what those 10,000 hours of deliberate practice do: They wire patterns and processes into long-term memory, allowing working memory to focus on new or unexpected challenges preprocessed through what's already in long-term memory.

Long-term memory gives us instant, fluid, "natural" reactions to events occurring around us. It deeply informs who we appear to be as we interact with the world. Consider this example:

A kindergarten student was watching the news on television with his grandfather when the initial bombing raids on Iraq were announced in 2003. As soon as a map showing the targets in Iraq came on the screen, the little boy turned to his grandfather and said, "Is *that* where they're bombing? Are they taking care of the old things?" His grandfather, bemused, asked him what old things he was talking about. "That's the Fertile Crescent—we've been studying it. It's where civilization started—there are many old things there. Grandpa, are they taking care of the old things?"

That lad's repeated exposure to the maps and history of the Fertile Crescent wired long-term memory to recognize those features and feed them to working memory, even in an unexpected situation. That's the point—what's stored in long-term memory changes how one views the world, allowing the mind to effortlessly make sense of new chunks. This is the intuition underlying University of Virginia Professor E. D. Hirsch's influential work on "cultural literacy."[11] The more a student has committed major historical and literary touchstones to long-term memory, the easier it is for her to make sense of new information and process new connections. Conversely, students who haven't mastered this same knowledge will have to struggle with the limitations of working memory when making sense of new information.

It's the relationship between working memory and long-term memory that determines whether tasks are "easy" or "hard" for learners. Things already stashed in long-term memory are perceived as "simple," or "obvious," because they are accessed without conscious effort. The more one masters in a given domain, the easier things are for working memory, and the less burdened it feels. On the other hand, when tackling a problem with little internalized long-term memory, everything gets processed through working memory. This creates overload, making everything slower, more effortful, and error-prone; kind of like running a computer with too many applications open.

Thus, a core challenge for instruction is building long-term memory so as to make it accessible and useful for working memory. We do this by having students work on tasks and make decisions that tax working memory. The repeated feedback and practice then build capacities into long-term memory.

Consider how this plays out in a typical classroom. The range of skills that various students have mastered in long-term memory varies widely: At any given point, some students are still learning what nouns are, while others are ready for the work of crafting compelling paragraphs. If a teacher is teaching students to write a strong topic sentence for a paragraph, some will find this a simple question of mastering one new chunk of information. Others will be swamped by a confusing mess of words.

Think about how someone learns to drive. At first, the most basic controls dominate working memory—"Which pedal slows it down, Daddy?"—leaving little room for much else. However, with repeated practice and feedback, what was slow and laborious gradually becomes familiar. New things can take up working memory—"Was I supposed to stop before turning left there, Daddy?" After more practice, even these decisions become automated—"Uh, wait, did I even drive by the movie theater on my way home from school today?"—leaving working memory free to tackle something completely different while driving—"Did you see what Paul wore to school today? OMG!" (much to her father's consternation).

The False Dichotomy

Understanding the relationship of working and long-term memory helps address the false dichotomy between "rote memory" and "conceptual understanding" that sometimes plagues discussion of pedagogy. Learners have to develop certain fast, fluent capabilities if they are to prepare for the next tier of learning—and "rote learning" can indeed be one effective tool for building some of this fluency. Ideological debates about learning have obscured the reality that students need enough repeated practice and feedback to build long-term memory, if they are to free room for working memory to tackle new tasks and challenges—and work toward deeper, more conceptual mastery. Absent repeated practice and feedback, students may be able to struggle through a task by leaning on working memory, but they'll never be more than moderately adept.

As students tackle more complicated tasks and concepts, those who have not absorbed key building blocks into long-term memory will find it hard to keep up. They'll tend to stall out. A lack of support in long-term memory means new things will ask too much of working memory. Compare the fluency of a teenager typing on a smartphone with that of her less practiced parents, who use such a device in a much more occasional, awkward, stumbling manner, as they struggle to "think through their fingers" in this tiny medium.

Now, as we've noted, experts routinely lose conscious track of what is in their long-term memory. Research shows that when experts train novices, they tend to leave out a lot of important information—70% or more of what's required to complete a task![12] It's not because the experts are trying to be difficult, it's just that they take for granted essential building blocks in long-term memory. They haven't had to think much about these things for years, making it easy to take important chunks of their own expertise for granted.

This is why experts may not always be the best instructors or designers of instruction. For instance, former superstar ballplayers, for whom fluid mastery came naturally, are often less suited to coaching than former teammates who mastered their craft much more deliberately and haltingly. Compared with superstars, those who struggle to achieve mastery are more conscious of what they do, the mistakes learners make, and the kinds of demonstration and practice that may help. A familiar example of this dynamic is the expert university professor who has trouble coherently teaching a freshman course.

When it comes to schooling, most teachers have been successful learners themselves, but, over time, many of the study skills, habits, and academic foundations that they've mastered have become invisible to them. One of the values of mentors or tutors is that they can help students focus on skills or knowledge that teachers might take for granted.

UNDERSTANDING WHAT EXPERTS DO

In the military or in large, well-managed companies like Cisco Systems, Inc., instructional designers interview subject-matter experts and work closely with them to develop instructional programs. Through careful questioning, the designer can identify more of what a novice needs to know. It turns out that this process works better if the instructional designer is not an expert herself, because she's more likely to ask the "stupid questions" that get at key underpinnings the learner needs.

"Cognitive task analysis" (CTA) is a more systematic way for interviewers to unpack experts' nonconscious expertise.[13] Evidence shows training built from such analyses can reduce learning time by 25% or more, and improve performance dramatically. For example, research has found that surgery residents trained with a CTA-based method outperformed a randomized control group of residents trained the conventional way.[14]

How to apply these techniques in schooling is an open question. One might do a CTA of successful college students to understand the full range of decisions and tasks they've mastered (especially when it comes to things like note-taking, organizing, and study skills), and then use that to identify instructional needs for K–12 students. Another possibility is to identify teachers who are exceptionally effective with certain types of students and do a CTA with an eye to modifying teacher training and support.

DELIBERATE PRACTICE

The natural limitations on working memory and the need for repeated practice with feedback make learning hard work. That's why research across many fields suggests that adult expertise flows from a huge amount (around 10,000 hours) of "deliberate practice."[15]

For example, Anders Ericsson and colleagues analyzed the lives of a range of violin students at the Music Academy of West Berlin, from those likely to be music teachers on up to those professors judged to have the highest potential to play professionally at an international level. The main difference: the number of hours they engaged in deliberate practice. The best students had accumulated their 10,000 hours of deliberate practice already at age 20, while less skilled students had accumulated only 4,000 hours.[16]

In his book *Talent Is Overrated*, Geoff Colvin describes a number of deliberate methods the young Benjamin Franklin used to become a better writer.[17] Franklin would read and summarize well-written essays, put the notes away, then try to rewrite the full essay based on his notes, which he would compare with the original to see where he had room to improve.

To force himself to master new words, Franklin started to rewrite the essays in verse. He would then rewrite the full essay in prose, from the verses. To master organization, he would take each note on a separate piece of paper and then scramble the sheets. He would wait a while, and then attempt to reorder his notes and use them to rewrite the essay. He would do all of this over and over again.

Yes, this can all seem incredibly tedious. On the other hand, Colvin points out that any of us could do this. It's just that few do. Scratching at the surface story of almost anyone who is extraordinarily good at something reveals a similar vast stock of repeated practice—often, of specifically designed training. That's as true of great movie directors, comedians, and baseball players as it is of great violinists, physicists, and playwrights.

"Deliberate practice" is not merely repeating what one has done before. It involves breaking a task into manageable components and then practicing each in an intentional, working-memory-intensive fashion, until a new level of routine competence is achieved. So how do we get there? Research suggests we can split expertise into the *procedures* to accomplish decisions and tasks and the *conceptual knowledge* that supports those procedures.[18] These two types require different kinds of practice.

Procedures are what it takes to get things done, whether that's writing a paper or designing a chemistry experiment. These become fluent, and nonconscious, as when someone who has mastered algebra hardly has to think at all about how to solve an equation. One important component that often becomes automatic is deciding *when* to do a procedure (e.g., "I've done enough research and am ready to start writing the paper"). Because nonconscious decisions about procedures can seem obvious to those who have already mastered them, teachers can find it easy to shortchange instruction on *how, when,* and *why* to apply supporting conceptual knowledge, focusing only on the raw conceptual knowledge itself.[19] Research suggests that the right way to teach procedures is to demonstrate the various steps, have students practice these and the application of conceptual knowledge within them, get immediate feedback on their performance, and then apply these skills through tasks that gradually grow in variety and complexity.[20]

Conceptual knowledge is the stuff you need to know to be able to carry out procedures. For instance, writers are supposed to write for an intended audience. Well, what's an "audience" in this context? That's something a student needs to learn. Conceptual knowledge includes facts, concepts, processes, and principles. Note that these elements sound a lot like what you might learn in school. What is easy to miss is the importance of helping students learn to *use* these things all together when performing procedures.

These distinctions in types of expertise matter because different kinds of practice are needed for each type. For example, it's no surprise that facts are efficiently taught through spaced repetition (recall that Ebbinghaus research from the 19th century we mentioned earlier). It turns out concepts, by themselves, are best mastered not by rote memorization, but by *using* them to classify things or situations: "This is a momentum problem; this is an energy problem." (A well-known study comparing experts' and novices' ability to solve mechanics problems in physics showed that experts classify such problems up-front in this way, while novices don't.[21]) However, the right way to teach an entire procedure is by having students do it in full, using all the supporting conceptual knowledge (facts, concepts, processes, principles) in the right way at the same time, and then getting feedback quickly on the whole performance.

WORKING MEMORY HAS TWO CHANNELS: AUDIO AND VISUAL

Our minds process audio and visual information on parallel tracks; this matters for learning. For instance, it makes a big difference whether instruction involves simultaneous delivery of *well-designed* audio and visuals as poorly designed audio can actually distract students and impede learning.[22] When carefully synchronized, instruction that uses both offers a turbo boost over visuals alone.

"Effect sizes" are how learning researchers compare the impact of interventions. They reflect how many "standard deviations" learning has moved. This can all sound complicated, but it's really pretty straightforward. A simple way to think about them: If you have a 50th percentile performer in your class, and you move the whole class by one standard deviation in performance (an "effect size" of one), you'll move that performer to the 84th percentile—a very large move, indeed. A gain of 1.5 standard deviations for the class means that the learner has moved to the 93rd percentile. These are obviously significant gains. (Most conventional educational interventions yield effect sizes that are a fraction of a standard deviation.)

Research shows that instruction that makes good use of both audio and visual learning yields very large benefits for learners. For instance, across nine studies, instruction that used both text and graphics together—rather than text alone—showed a 1.5 standard deviation improvement in learning. Across 20 studies listening to an audio version of text instead of reading it improved learning by almost one standard deviation. The way you go about this matters: Across 11 studies getting rid of cluttered text and irrelevant images resulted in a 1.3 standard deviation improvement.[23]

Cluttering either the visual or audio channel with extraneous information, graphics, or sound overtaxes working memory and makes it harder to learn. This is why someone reading a presentation off of PowerPoint slides can be so frustrating (not to mention dull). They are forcing working memory to process the same information twice, bogging it down as it compares the slides and the narration and noting small differences. (Clark and Mayer report that this kind of presentation produces a median *decrease* in learning of almost 0.7 standard deviations, dropping the median performer down to the 25th percentile.[24])

It may not be as sexy as 3-D simulations and virtual reality games, but getting this stuff right can make a huge difference, saving resources while supporting learning. At the same time, getting it wrong can cause learning to plummet. This is where thinking like a learning engineer can pay huge dividends.

THE CRUCIAL ROLE OF STUDENT MOTIVATION

You can lead a horse to water without its drinking a drop. Similarly, the kinds of instructional elements just discussed make a difference only if students are motivated to learn. Indeed, research suggests that 30%–40% of learning performance is a question of whether a student values the task and thinks she can master it.[25]

Let's be clear about what "motivation" means in this context. We often hear that schools should spend a mint on tablets, laptops, or mobile devices because "kids today love technology." We hear about technology's miraculous powers to charm students, as with the excitable Texas middle-school teacher who told the local press: "I'll stop and say, 'Get out your computers,' and you see the light in their eyes. It's just magic."[26] Heck, sometimes new learning approaches are sold with the assurance, "They won't even know they're learning!" Trust us—if the topic is challenging and significant, like writing a persuasive essay or solving problems with ratios and proportions, kids will know they're learning. They're unlikely to ever confuse such tasks with a massive multi-player fantasy role-playing game or watching ribald smartphone footage, even when the practice entails well-designed, technology-enhanced learning.

In truth, "liking" may not matter as much as you might think. People routinely work hard at activities they don't "like" if they find them useful and rewarding. Just think of athletes in weight rooms or at basketball camp, dancers at the barre, or musicians working their scales. If you ask those athletes, dancers, or musicians if they "like" the activity, many will say, "No!" But they do it, and many do it willingly, even eagerly. Why? Because practice is key to getting good at something—and they know it.

Cognitive scientists define motivation to mean the willingness to start something, keep at it, and work hard at it. They're much less concerned with whether someone "likes" it.[27] When learning is well-designed and valuable, learners can be motivated to see it through, even if it's not their favorite thing.

In fact, research in learning warns that what students "like" isn't necessarily what will help them learn best. For example, researchers compared three methods of studying for a test on science content: rereading the material in a textbook, mapping the concepts, and having students repeatedly write summaries of what they read. Researchers found that the archaic idea of summarizing and writing (remember Ben Franklin?) worked better than the more fashionable concept-mapping technique, and both worked better than simply rereading the text. Just as interesting, however, was that, when surveyed about which approach they thought would help the most, most students said reading the text and the fewest said repeated summarization. This was exactly the opposite of what the evidence showed would boost learning.[28]

Another study asked novices to indicate whether they preferred a high- or a low-practice environment for learning and then randomly assigned them to one or the other. Regardless of what they thought they'd prefer, the students in the high-practice environment did better.[29] Another study compared student ratings of a professor's likability to student learning; the researchers found remarkably low correlations (ranging from 0.12 to 0.15) between whether students "liked" their professor and how much they learned.[30]

Kaplan University conducted a controlled trial of an attempt to revise virtual college-level courses using learning science.[31] Teachers used data to target their instruction, incorporated more real-world practice, and so on. The results were promising, with higher retention in subsequent courses, improved performance, higher grades, and more time spent on learning. However, it turned out that the students liked the new courses *less* than the originals. This sounds puzzling. The students did better, worked harder, and were more likely to stay in the new courses—but didn't *like* the courses as much? Looking at student feedback helped clarify things: Students said they worked harder in these courses than in their more traditional ones. Thus, when asked their "likes", they answered with an eye to the increased workload. This didn't stop them from doing the work, doing better, and learning more. Put simply, student preferences don't necessarily align with what will help them learn.

This dichotomy between what we "like" and what's good for us crops up in every walk of life—just think about choosing between chocolate and broccoli. Heck, we don't expect the physician to ask the 6-year-old patient if he'd "like" a vaccine shot. It's up to the educators to design powerful learning environments and not to default to convention or what students say they like. And it's crucial not to be taken in by vendors who insist their products work *because* students are sure to love them. Don't get us wrong—we want experiences to be as enjoyable as possible. However, the real motivation that drives learning isn't just about liking stuff.

More usefully, research points to at least four kinds of problems that can hamper motivation and hinder learning. Let's touch on each.

Valuing problems happen when a learner doesn't see the point of an activity. The solution is to demonstrate why the learner should value the activity or goal. This could entail showing how the immediate goal fits in with larger interests or career goals. It can also involve having people with goals and backgrounds similar to the learner's talk about how this goal or activity made a difference for them.[32]

Self-efficacy problems happen when a learner believes he or she cannot do a task ("I'm no good at math"). This is different from a valuing problem because the learner may well know that the objective is useful but doesn't believe she can accomplish it. For learners with low self-efficacy, it's vital to communicate an unshakable confidence that the learner can successfully master the objective. A promising strategy could entail breaking up the problem into smaller chunks, changing the nature and frequency of practice and feedback, and sharing stories of others who, like the learner, thought they couldn't do the task but did.[33]

Attribution problems are similar to self-efficacy problems, but happen when learners blame their lack of progress on external factors they believe they cannot control. For example, a student might say, "It's impossible for me to learn from this book," or, "There's no way I can learn from that teacher." The solution is similar to that for self-efficacy: conveying an unshakable conviction that the learner can succeed, and then helping the learner strategize ways to conquer the perceived problem.[34]

Emotion or mood problems happen when learners are angry, scared, or depressed about the topic, the class, or their lives. Such negative emotions can emerge as the complexity of a learning task increases.[35] These emotions may prevent learners from getting started or persisting at challenging tasks. Actions that counter negative emotions—such as positive teachers and role models—have been found to help restore motivation.[36]

So it's not enough to design learning environments that *would* succeed "if only students would get to work." Learning engineers also have to think intentionally about what in the learning environment will motivate learners to start, persist, and put in effort.

PUTTING LEARNING SCIENCE TO WORK

Let's recap: Our minds work by combining slow, flexible, conscious processing of working memory with fast, fluent, parallel tools and information from long-term memory. As more capabilities are mastered in long-term memory, working memory uses those to tackle new, challenging tasks. Learning scientists now know a great deal about the types of practice that build long-term memory, how media can help or hinder learning, and how problems with motivation can get in the way of learning.

With all this known, why isn't more of the research getting used?

Let's be clear. Many effective learning environments exhibit these evidence-based principles in various ways—and successful teachers, schools, and tutors intuitively employ these ideas in their own practices.

For example, Doug Lemov's huge-selling 2010 book *Teach Like a Champion* is so useful because it identifies specific practices that work in classrooms.[37] Lemov makes no claim that he's drawing on learning science, but he's a savvy, smart, and observant educator who has noted practices common to many terrific teachers. It shouldn't be a surprise that many of the principles Lemov describes dovetail nicely with what we might predict from the learning sciences. Some examples:

- "Name the steps": The best teachers take complex materials, break them down, and make the steps visible to students. They then teach each step and finally teach how to solve new problems using all the steps. For example, they emphasize taking time to be very systematic about the different steps required to write a persuasive essay, and practicing each one, before putting them all together. All this meshes neatly with what we know from learning science.
- "No opt-out": Exceptional teachers do not give up on students, even when students are saying "I don't know" or "I can't do this." These teachers make it a point to not let students settle into a convenient, tranquil apathy. They use other students' responses to prompt the frustrated students, break problems into their component parts, and refuse to allow the student to believe they cannot do the problem. This parallels what we know about motivation and also deliberate practice: Listening is not enough.
- "Do not engage": Effective teachers don't engage in distracting talk with a student in the middle of class. They keep conversation directed to learning goals and not other things. For instance, they don't let a conversation about fractions turn into a critique of the textbook. This is a nice application of the limited capacity of working memory— bouncing amidst multiple topics will cause students to lose the thread of instruction, impeding learning and practice.

What does learning science have to add to all this? Well, it provides grounding that can help leaders systematize these intuitions and make sense of a noisy mass of ideas. Educators aren't always clear on why suggestions might work, or why a vendor's new offering might disappoint, or how to translate successful practices from one environment into another. The result: Opportunities are missed, or bad ideas become conventional wisdom. That's where learning science can help.

SEVEN ELEMENTS OF LEARNING

We know we've covered a lot of ground in a hurry. Just to make sure we're all on the same page, let's take a moment to consider how learning science applies to a typical unit of instruction. The seven elements are all painfully familiar: overview, information, demonstrations, practice and feedback, assessment, outcomes/objectives, and motivation support. Every teacher engages with these elements when teaching, and every administrator looks for them when observing a class. We'll illustrate how learning science applies to each when helping students learn to craft syntheses of longer essays, a skill that both Ben Franklin and current research suggest is useful for young writers.[38]

Objectives: Objectives come first. They are the things we want students to learn to do. Objectives need to be concrete (so that students and teachers know when the objective has been mastered); current

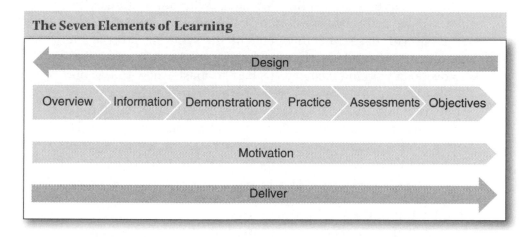

The Seven Elements of Learning

Design

Overview Information Demonstrations Practice Assessments Objectives

Motivation

Deliver

(focused on the present—not the distant future); and challenging (to maximize learning). Clear objectives help clarify the purpose of the learning, providing motivation through value, and they lend structure to what's being taught, helping with limited working memory. In our writing example, the objective might be, "The learner will be able to write a clear, brief synthesis of a persuasive essay that includes the main points, characteristics of the expected audience, and the argument and evidence used." This is specific, about behaviors, and signals what the assessment should address.

Assessments: Assessments gauge current expertise for a given objective. They tend to work best when tapping into authentic performances that entail both procedural and conceptual knowledge. That's why we feel more confident if we see how student drivers perform on an actual road and not merely on a test of driving knowledge. To ensure assessments measure the intended knowledge or skills, they should be tightly coupled to the objective. Indeed, when the objective is clear enough, assessment is simple. Here, the assessment involves students penning syntheses of persuasive essays. In our example, multiple choice questions would not suffice—we want students to produce written syntheses with clarity, organization, and depth.

Practice and corrective feedback: Practice should be clearly linked and aligned to learning objectives and assessment. Optimally, practice and corrective feedback amount to interactive versions of "formative" assessment. In other words, students practice key tasks and get real-time feedback. With our writing example, it'd be natural to have students synthesize sets of essays, starting with different components of the synthesis process and then eventually tackling the exercise in its entirety. Since it's easy to overload working memory, it's best to master new things one deliberate step at a time. We should start with simpler essays, so that we don't overload students trying to decipher the various texts, and then raise the difficulty level as mastery grows. As instructional differentiation advises, students' practice ought to be modified to account for varying skills and starting points.

Demonstrations: Research suggests that showing well-constructed demonstrations before students start to practice helps them cement their sense of what mastery entails.[39] "Worked examples," which start as demonstrations, evolving into guided practice and then solo practice, are a powerful tool, as they let students learn the elements of mastery and then learn to apply them. Giving students control over the pace of their work can enable them to slow down, speed up, review, and repeat the material in a fashion that helps them reach mastery.[40] In demonstrating how a good synthesis is written, we might show an essay, then a good synthesis, and then talk through the steps that produced the synthesis. We might show various drafts of the work that led to the final product, with clear commentary connecting what's changed and why.

Information: To maximize the value of demonstrations and practice, learners need a certain amount of information ahead of time. To conserve working memory and avoid distractions, information should be as simple and focused as possible, and presented in discrete chunks. These ought to be immediately used in demonstrations and practice to cement context and familiarity. It's a mistake to present large blocks of information before students get to apply any of it. When subjects are difficult and complex, effective instruction breaks them up into finer slices and then uses visual and auditory media to help working memory absorb the new information. For our writing synthesis example, we might provide an audio and visual review of key steps: initially focusing on the title, first paragraph, and last paragraph of the original essay, then tackling the rest of the essay to flesh out the argument being made and the evidence being used, and finally working to pen the synthesis itself from an outline and notes.

Overview: An initial overview of the whole learning activity provides a structure and a chance to explain why the objective and practice are important. The former helps with working memory, while the latter encourages motivation. Good overviews link the unit to what learners have learned before, in and out of class. For our writing synthesis lessons, we might talk about the value of summarizing arguments to developing counterarguments and providing applied examples (such as why parents should have allowed students to attend that concert last weekend). We might even briefly mention the research suggesting that doing syntheses helps make one a better writer—it's going to be real work for the learners, so we should try to demonstrate its value.

Motivation support: When topics are challenging, motivation is critical. While the overview can help, motivation needs to be supported throughout a learning activity. Teachers benefit from knowing when specific motivation failures occur and being able to obtain real-time guidance on what to do about it. Valuable motivation supports include useful, real-time feedback; demonstrating the importance of topics; and sharing success stories and strategies from learners with similar challenges. For those students who insist, "I just can't write," there's no substitute for a committed teacher affirming that they can do this work, sharing examples of others who had difficulties writing but got good at it, and breaking down the tasks into manageable, confidence-building, working memory–friendly pieces.

We'll occasionally return to these seven elements, as they provide an essential framework for thinking about when and how to redesign schools or classrooms—with or without technology.

RESOURCES ON LEARNING SCIENCE

For those aspiring learning engineers hoping to learn more, here are a few key resources to get you started:

Why Students Don't Like School by Daniel Willingham. This is an immensely readable summary of how cognitive science should inform teaching practices. Willingham has been answering teachers' questions about learning for years in the American Federation of Teachers newsletter, and this book distills his considerable wisdom.[41]

Talent Is Overrated by Geoffrey Colvin. Another easy read, Colvin's book explores the foundations of expertise and what's required to achieve it. Colvin focuses on the role and nature of "deliberate practice." A business writer for *Fortune* magazine, Colvin peppers his writing with popular examples.[42]

E-Learning and the Science of Instruction by Ruth Clark and Richard Mayer. This is a detailed survey of how learning science can guide instruction. Don't be fooled by the title—the evidence and implications here can be applied in paper-and-pencil environments as easily as online ones.[43]

First Principles of Instruction by David Merrill. Merrill is one of the finest instructional designers in the world, and has spent decades working to incorporate cognitive science research into instructional design. This is a crystal-clear synthesis of how to apply his principles.[44]

How People Learn, edited by John Bransford, Ann Brown, and Rodney Cocking. A synthesis of decades of learning research up through 2000, this volume provides a remarkable overview of the literature and a strong foundation for making sense of more recent discoveries.[45]

"Design Factors for Educationally Effective Animations and Simulations" by Jan Plass, Bruce Homer, and Elizabeth Hayward. An excellent review of research about animations and simulations, discussing what works and what doesn't. While this is a fast-moving area of inquiry, Plass, Homer, and Hayward provide a terrific framework for evaluating new media for learning.[46]

"The Implications of Research on Expertise for Curriculum and Pedagogy" by David Feldon. An eye-opening exploration of nonconscious expertise and why experts often fail to design or deliver instruction for novices in ways that will help them succeed. Feldon's analysis challenges our conventional assumption that experts naturally make the best instructors.[47]

IES Practice Guides. Produced by the U.S. Department of Education's Institute of Education Sciences, these guides offer invaluable research distillations and evidence-based recommendations on an array of topics, including math and reading instruction, helping girls stay engaged with science and math, and dropout prevention.[48]

National Math Advisory Panel reports. These reports resulted from a major U.S. Department of Education effort to synthesize the best research on math instruction and offer guidelines for practice. Math educators will find these materials very helpful, especially the *Report of the Task Force on Learning Processes.* [49]

Pittsburgh Science of Learning Center (PSLC). The PSLC is a federally funded research center jointly run by the University of Pittsburgh and Carnegie Mellon University. It's a world leader when it comes to integrating learning science, technology-enhanced instruction, and "big data" to improve teaching and learning. The website is a rich resource, and PSLC runs summer institutes on a variety of topics.[50]

A FEW KEY TAKEAWAYS

We know there's a lot to keep in mind, so let's try to distill some of the key takeaways:

- Expertise takes both fast, fluent, nonconscious work by long-term memory and conscious, more deliberate processing of complex challenges by working memory. Long-term memory assists working memory, though we don't even notice—because things that draw on long-term memory typically seem effortless.
- Learning new things is tough because it requires disciplined feedback—and the only way to build long-term memory is by deeply engaging working memory.
- Because minds define "simple" based on what's stored in long-term memory, the same activity may seem "simple" to one mind and "confusing" to another. That's why you need to personalize instruction to optimize learning.
- Experts have so much wired into their long-term memories that their judgment on what's "easy" and "hard" can be unreliable. We have to be very deliberate about designing instruction and use data on student progress to refine it.
- Motivation to learn is different from "liking" what you're doing. Getting motivation right is critical for learning—identifying what's really wrong (valuing, self-efficacy, attribution, emotion) and treating the specific problem are key.
- Every part of a learning unit (the outcomes, assessment, practice and feedback, demonstrations, information, overviews, and motivation support) can be done in ways that either accelerate or hinder learning.

When it comes to putting these ideas to work, there isn't one obvious answer. The lesson is not to seek out magic recipes but to approach teaching and learning with eyes wide open. R. Keith Sawyer, associate professor of education at Washington University, suggests, "Learning sciences research explains why the promise of computers in schools has not yet been realized . . . [and] suggests that the computer should take on a more facilitating role, helping learners have the kind of experiences that lead to deep learning."[51]

As we'll discuss in Chapter 3, learning science can provide invaluable guidance for thinking about how technology can help learners master skills and knowledge, explore big questions, and stimulate their minds in better, cheaper, faster ways. Tech-enabled school design provides the opportunity to leverage the insights of learning science in increasingly powerful ways. How do we do that?

NOTES

1. Gelineau, K. (2012, December 10). Gov't: Building felled by NZ quake poorly built. Associated Press. Retrieved from http://abcnews.go.com; Stewart, A., Wright, M., & Greenhill, M. (2012). "I just want justice." Fairfax New Zealand Limited. Retrieved from http://www.stuff.co.nz/

2. Sawyer, R. K. (2006). *The Cambridge handbook of the learning sciences.* New York, NY: Cambridge University Press. pp. 3,15

3. Fields, R. D. (2008). White matter in learning, cognition and psychiatric disorders. *Trends in Neurosciences 31*(7), 361–370.

4. Aylward, E. H., Richards, T. L, Berninger, V. W., Nagy, W. E., Field, K. M., Grimme, A. C., & Cramer, S. C. (2003). Instructional treatment associated with changes in brain activation in children with dyslexia. *Neurology, 61,* 212–219.

5. Kolata, G. (2012). Study divides breast cancer into four distinct types. *New York Times.* Retrieved from http://www.nytimes.com

6. Ebbinghaus, H. (1885). *Memory: A contribution to experimental psychology.* New York, NY: Teachers College Press.

7. Clark, R. C., & Mayer, R. E. (2011). *E-Learning and the science of instruction* (3rd ed.). San Francisco, CA: Pfeiffer.

8. Ericsson, K. A, Krampe, R. Th., & Tesch-Romer, C. (1993). The role of deliberate practice in the acquisition of expert performance. *Psychological Review, 100*(3), 363–406.

9. Clark, R. C., Mayer, R. E. (2011). *E-Learning and the science of instruction* (3rd ed.). San Francisco, CA: Pfeiffer; Glaser, R. (1990). The reemergence of learning theory within instructional research. *American Psychologist, 45,* 29–39; Schneider, W., & Chein, J. M. (2003). Controlled and automatic processing: behavior, theory, and biological mechanisms. *Cognitive Science, 27,* 525–559.

10. Cowan, N. (2001). The magical number 4 in short-term memory: A reconsideration of mental storage capacity. *Behavioral and Brain Sciences, 24,* 87–114.

11. Hirsch, E. D. Jr. (1988). *Cultural literacy: What every American needs to know.* Boston, MA: Houghton Mifflin.
12. Feldon, D. F., & Clark, R. E. (2006). Instructional implications of cognitive task analysis as a method for improving the accuracy of experts' self-report. In G. Clarebout & J. Elen (Eds.), *Avoiding simplicity, confronting complexity: Advances in studying and designing (computer-based) powerful learning environments,* pp. 109–116, Rotterdam, The Netherlands: Sense Publishers.
13. Feldon, D. F., & Clark, R. E. (2006). Instructional implications of cognitive task analysis as a method for improving the accuracy of experts' self-report. In G. Clarebout & J. Elen (Eds.), *Avoiding simplicity, confronting complexity: Advances in studying and designing (computer-based) powerful learning environments,* pp.109–116, Rotterdam, The Netherlands: Sense Publishers.
14. Velmahos, G. C., Toutouzas, K.G., Sillin, L. F., Chan L., Clark R. E., Theodorou, D., & Maupin, F. (2004). Cognitive task analysis for teaching technical skills in an inanimate surgical skills laboratory. *The American Journal of Surgery, 187,* 114–119.
15. Colvin, G. (2010). *Talent is overrated: What really separates world-class performers from everybody else.* New York, NY: Portfolio Trade.
16. Ericsson, K. A., Krampe, R. T., & Tesch-Romer, C. (1993). The role of deliberate practice in the acquisition of expert performance. *Psychological Review, (100)*3, 363–406.
17. Colvin, G. (2010). *Talent is overrated: What really separates world-class performers from everybody else.* New York, NY: Portfolio Trade.
18. Koedinger, K. R., Corbett, A. T., & Perfettio, C. (2010). The knowledge-learning-instruction (KLI) framework: Toward bridging the science-practice chasm to enhance robust student learning. *Carnegie Mellon University Technical Report.* Available at http://www.learnlab.org/opportunities/summer/readings/PSLC-Theory-Framework-Tech-Rep.pdf
19. Clark, R. C., & Mayer, R. E. (2011). *E-learning and the science of instruction* (3rd ed.). San Francisco, CA: Pfeiffer.
20. Sweller, J., Ayres P., & Kalyuga, S. (2011). *Cognitive load theory.* New York, NY: Springer.
21. Chi, M. T. H., Glaser, R., & Reese, E. (1982). Expertise in problem solving. In R. J. Sternberg (Ed.), *Advances in the psychology of human intelligence,* 1: 7–76. Hillsdale, NJ: Lawrence Erlbaum Associates.
22. Clark, R. C., & Mayer, R. E. (2011). *E-learning and the science of instruction* (3rd ed.). San Francisco, CA: Pfeiffer.

23. Clark, R. C., & Mayer, R. E. (2011). *E-learning and the science of instruction* (3rd ed.). San Francisco, CA: Pfeiffer, p. 403.

24. Clark, R. C., & Mayer, R. E. (2011). *E-Learning and the science of instruction* (3rd ed.). San Francisco, CA: Pfeiffer.

25. Colquitt, J. A., LePine, J. A., & Noe, R. A. (2000). Toward an integrative theory of training motivation: A meta-analytic path analysis of 20 years of research. *Journal of Applied Psychology, 85*(5), 678–707.

26. Kastner, L. (2012, November 26). Laptops, iPads piquing students' interest. *San Antonio Express-News.* Section A, p. 12. Retrieved from http://www.lexisnexis.com

27. Schunk, D. H., Pintrich, P. R., & Meece, J. L. (2007). *Motivation in education: Theory, research and applications* (3rd ed.). Pearson Education Inc.

28. Karpicke J. D., & Blunt, J. R. (2011, January 20). Retrieval practice produces more learning than elaborative studying with concept mapping. *Science, 331*(6018), 317.

29. Karpicke J.D., & Blunt, J.R. (2011, January 20). Retrieval practice produces more learning than elaborative studying with concept mapping. *Science, 331*(6018), 317.

30. Clark, R.C., & Mayer, R.E. (2011). *E-Learning and the science of instruction* (3rd ed.). San Francisco, CA: Pfeiffer

31. Sugrue, B., Ellefsen, E., Garry, S., & Williams, L. (2012, April 15). *Investigating the value of evidence-based instructional design for online university courses.* Paper presented as part of a symposium, Cognitive science goes to college: scaling up what we know about learning and instruction, at the annual meeting of the American Educational Research Association, Vancouver, Canada.

32. Eccles. J., & Wigfield, A. (2002). Motivational beliefs, values and goals. *Annual Review of Psychology, 53,* 109–132.

33. Bandura, A. (1997). *Self efficacy: The exercise of control.* New York, NY: W. H. Freeman.

34. Weiner, B. (1986). *An attributional theory of motivation and emotion.* New York, NY: Springer.

35. Clark, R.E., Howard, K., & Early, S. (2006). Motivational challenges in complex environments. In J. Elen & R. E. Clark (Eds.), *Handling complexity in learning environments: Research and theory.* Oxford, UK: Elsevier. p. 32.

36. Pekrun, R., Goetz, W. T., & Perry, R. P. (2002). Academic emotions in students' self-regulated learning and achievement: A program of

qualitative and quantitative research. *Educational Psychologist, 37*(2), 91–95; Bandura, A. (1997). *Self-efficacy: The exercise of control.* New York: W. H. Freeman.

37. Lemov, D. (2010). *Teach like a champion.* San Francisco, CA: Jossey-Bass.
38. Graham, S., & Perin, D. (2007). *Writing next: Effective strategies to improve writing of adolescents in middle and high schools—A report to Carnegie Corporation of New York.* Washington, DC: Alliance for Excellent Education.
39. Sweller, J., Ayres P., & Kalyuga, S. (2011). *Cognitive load theory.* New York, NY: Springer.
40. Clark, R. C., & Mayer, R. E. (2011). *E-Learning and the science of instruction* (3rd ed.). San Francisco, CA: Pfeiffer.
41. Willingham, D. (2010). *Why students don't like school?* San Francisco, CA: Jossey-Bass.
42. Colvin, G. (2010). *Talent is overrated: What really separates world-class performers from everybody else.* New York, NY: Portfolio.
43. Clark, R. C., & Mayer, R. E. (2011). *E-learning and the science of instruction* (3rd ed.). San Francisco, CA: Pfeiffer.
44. Merrill, D. (2009). First principles of instruction. In C. M Reigeluth & A. Carr (Eds.), *Instructional design theories and models III.* New York, NY: Routledge.
45. Bransford, J., Brown, A., & Cocking, R. (Eds.). (2000). *How people learn: Brain, mind, experience, and school.* Washington, DC: National Academy Press.
46. Plass, J. L., Homer, B. D., & Hayward, E. (2009). Design factors for educationally effective animations and simulations. *Journal of Computing in Higher Education, 21*(1), 31–61.
47. Feldon, D. (2007). The implications of research on expertise for curriculum and pedagogy. *Education Psychology Review, 19,* 91–110.
48. Practice guides are available at http://ies.ed.gov/ncee/wwc/publi cations_reviews.aspx, using keyword "practice guide."
49. More information about the National Advisory Panel Reports can be found at http://www2.ed.gov/about/bdscomm/list/mathpanel/ index.html.
50. To learn more about the Pittsburgh Science of Learning Center, visit http://www.learnlab.org.
51. Sawyer, R. K. (2006). *The Cambridge handbook of the learning sciences.* New York, NY: Cambridge University Press. p. 8.

CHAPTER 3

Applying Learning Science to Technology

Learning science can and should inform instruction, whether or not technology is involved. But new technologies create powerful new opportunities to leverage learning science.

What do we have in mind? Let's start with one of the simpler educational technologies: your genial chalkboard (which has mostly given way to your genial marker-friendly whiteboard or high-tech smartboard). We're so familiar with the primitive chalkboard that we rarely think of it as technology—it's just "what teachers used back when."

But it's a mistake to be so dismissive. The humble chalkboard enabled teachers to do things they couldn't do without it. It allowed them to keep notes; to have students come up and do work that the whole class could inspect; to share large, ad hoc diagrams and drawings; and to track student ideas or the flow of a class discussion. It provided a visual complement to the teacher's audio voice-over—in response to student questions and concerns—and offered a reviewable track of material covered in the lesson.

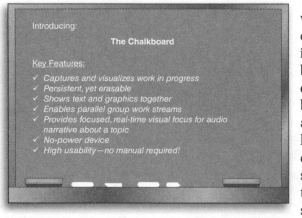

And that's before we encounter the once-remarkable innovation of *sliding* blackboards that drop down one behind another, as in an old-school college lecture hall. These can be used to reveal surprising information, show completed solutions, pose pre-planned problems . . . hold us back! OK, you might not share our enthusiasm (and maybe we really should get out more). But you get the idea.

Now, consider the smartboard. What do smartboards let educators do that's better or different from what they could do with chalkboards? Well, smartboards allow teachers to pre-store whole series of diagrams or writings, and allow students to interact at the board with their teacher and classmates. They allow teachers to summon new information quickly from the Internet and show it to the class. These are all good and useful things.

But before deciding that the smartboard has upended the classroom, let's consider each of its uses in turn. The pre-storing of slides/diagrams is something that can be done with chalkboards, too: sliding boards do the same thing, just not as easily or well. Smartboards make slides easier to display and manipulate, but teachers have been showing pictures to students for centuries. Smartboards make it easier to put up examples of student work and to do it in real time—but teachers have long showed student essays on overheads or had students solve problems on a blackboard. Smartboards make it easier to summon new information from the Internet, but let's not forget that teachers have long been able to consult an encyclopedia (virtual or not) the night before if they sought a new factual nugget to share.

Don't get us wrong. Smartboards are great. They let educators do things better. It's just that most of what they allow isn't actually new. As Patrick Larkin, assistant superintendent in Burlington, Massachusetts, and a winner of the 2012 Digital Principal Award from the National Association of Secondary School Principals, explains, "We've always done a lot of the things that we're now doing with technology."

Chalkboards or smartboards can be used to execute both good and bad learning solutions. Too many fancy illustrations can overwhelm students, leaving them confused. A teacher might provide too many answers or cues too quickly, preventing students from actually working through problems on their own.

THE FIVE CAPABILITIES OF TECHNOLOGY

Even simple technologies don't automatically help learning. What matters is how the technology is used. Put simply, technology can make a (good or bad) new or old learning solution more *affordable, reliable, available, customizable,* and *data-rich.* Let's take these in turn.

Technology can make the delivery of solutions more *affordable* than before. Indeed, technology has brought tremendous disruption in other industries by completely changing cost structures. Look at the music industry, where record companies struggled to deal with cheap music via iTunes, MP3 downloads, and the rest. Or the challenges faced by a newspaper industry buffeted by ubiquitous Internet access and the fact that just about anyone can cheaply and easily launch a website.

Technology makes delivery more *reliable.* The best entertainment (music, dance, sports, and more) is now readily available via technology. With recorded performances, there are no schedule hassles, travel problems, or performer illness issues. A digitally mastered version of a concerto or popular song is now available with a mouse-click. Appliances, cars, medical care—all have become much more consistent as a result of technology components that have been designed to invariably do certain things a certain way, repeatedly.

Technology makes more things more *available.* The same machine-engineered parts for a broken-down car can easily be ordered and shipped anywhere in the country. Online customer service is available 24 hours a day. By clicking a button, you can order new electronics on a holiday or check out old episodes of *I Dream of Jeannie* at midnight. Without technology, think of all we'd miss: Up-close viewing of the beluga whale would be the province of a few hardy adventurers or the enormously rich. Few of us would see the World Series or the parachuting Queen of England at the Olympics. We might read about these (although newsprint, too, is a technology) or hear about them from someone who was there, but we'd miss the closer, more visceral experience offered by modern communications, recording, and photography.

Technology makes delivery more *customizable.* Amazon, Pandora, and Google use technology to customize the information and recommendations we receive. Sure, back in the day, the local shopkeeper whom you saw every week would set aside just the right pork chop for you, or keep back your favorite magazine before the new issue sold out. Before Internet-based travel, one of us flew so frequently between Los Angeles and Washington, DC on one airline that the ticket counter folks would print out his boarding pass as soon as they saw him in line. This kind of human-customized touch is now rare for most of us—it's too expensive, and we're too mobile. However, technology can step in and offer a pretty decent substitute that's available, reliable, and customizable based on prior behaviors and choices.

Finally, technology can make experiences more *data-rich.* Think of Amazon customizing suggestions based on your past purchases. Amazon and similar companies keep learning how to improve what they do because of the rich data at their disposal. Developers accelerate their knowledge of how we use technology by looking at the streams of information that our actions generate. This allows them to learn about what works, what isn't used, and what we're actually doing with our expensive gadgets.

When a great solution is combined with the advantages of technology, great things are possible. Teaching and learning haven't yet had their *Dark Side of the Moon* or *Avatar* moment—an amazing, transforming, technology-delivered, mass experience that resonates through many lives. (OK, *Sesame Street* is nothing to sneeze at, but still.) That's quite normal. When the movie camera was first developed, it was stuck on a stage recording an entire play from a fixed position—useful enough, but it took years before anyone realized the new technology made it possible to tell stories in much richer, more dynamic ways. We're still at the "camera on the stage" phase of technology for learning, but, as we'll see shortly, there are glimmers of possibility in the air.

THE TUTORING CHALLENGE

While we don't think education has yet benefited all that much from the amazing new technologies of the past quarter century, we do think the potential for radical rethinking looms large. What do we have in mind? One-to-one tutoring with a good tutor is about the best way we know to provide intense instruction, real-time customized assessment, and intensive, personalized practice. But it is typically far too expensive to provide at scale.

Technology can help with that. Kurt VanLehn, professor of computer science and engineering at Arizona State University, has reviewed more than 80 studies comparing "intelligent" (e.g., computer-based) tutoring systems to each other and to traditional tutoring, and found that these systems do pretty well.[1] Human tutors seem to be able to move groups of students by about 0.75 standard deviations (remember, this translates to moving the median students from the 50th percentile up to the 77th percentile . . . a pretty good move!). The simplest intelligent tutoring systems, those that provide feedback based on whether students got the answer right or wrong, offer about half as much benefit—0.36 standard deviations (moving the median student to the 64th percentile). More complex systems that provide guidance at each step of a problem start to get pretty close to the benefits of human tutoring—boosting student achievement by about 0.7 standard deviations (and lifting the median student to the 76th percentile). Interestingly, the most complex systems don't yet seem to provide any additional benefit beyond that.

VanLehn's analysis shows that the best of these systems can nearly match the performance of human tutors when it comes to helping students build skills. This isn't magic: What these systems are doing reflects the tenets of learning science. They provide targeted feedback, repeated practice, pacing matched to the student, a variety of illustrations and explanations as needed, and audio and visual channels of information. They're most likely not going to be as good as the very best human tutors—but they can approximate what typical human tutors do, at scale.

If these tutoring systems aren't any better than human tutors, why bother with them? Because these tutoring systems are always available, don't get tired or sick, never have a bad day, and accurately tell you how things are going. Technology can deliver scalable, cheap-to-deliver *good* solutions that do some things nearly as well as the average human tutor (if not the very best ones). And these systems have the potential to generate large amounts of performance data that can be used to systematically improve them. In short, they can make quality tutoring more affordable, reliable, available, customizable, and data-rich—providing real benefits and real learning solutions at scale.

Think about the practical challenges of tutoring. Houston Independent School District (HISD), for instance, uses hundreds of tutors for its Apollo 20 program. The district pays tutors $20,000 a year, plus benefits, yielding a total cost of around $25,000 per tutor.[2] Each tutor assists about 15 to 20 students a day, working with two students at a time. This means the cost of providing two-to-one tutoring for each participating student is about $1,000 to $1,500 per year. The resulting total cost of the program runs to millions of dollars each year to provide tutoring to just a tiny percentage of Houston's 200,000 students.[3] If tutoring were extended to serve even one in five students, the program would prove unaffordable.

It's not just the cash. Even with just 20 participating schools, HISD has difficulty recruiting and retaining the many talented tutors it needs. Imagine trying to recruit enough educated talent to serve hundreds, thousands, or millions of children—especially in communities where there may not be enough quality tutors to go around.

Adaptive, intelligent tutoring systems *are* expensive to build—but they suddenly look cheap when compared to the labor costs estimated above. For example, staff at the Open Learning Initiative at Carnegie Mellon University estimate that there's a one-time cost of hundreds of thousands of dollars to build one of its "cognitive tutor" adaptive learning environments to provide customized help for students in a course. Once running, though, the recurring costs are minimal. Contrast that with the millions of dollars *per year* it costs to meet a fraction of the need in Houston.

KNOW WHAT PROBLEM YOU'RE SOLVING

Many years ago, one of us worked in management consulting. Hearing a CEO say something like, "Well, I'm not sure what's wrong here, but let's buy a software package that can fix it," was a sure sign the company was in trouble. Executives who didn't really understand their predicaments with manufacturing or supply-chain costs would make the mistake of hoping that some fancy software would "get this under control." Truth is, good solutions have a lot more to do with solving problems than buying a new information management system. If the executives figured the problem out, they could often solve it without the expensive software. Conversely, a focus on buying new technology could easily serve as a distraction.

When decision makers don't understand the problem they're solving, technology-based solutions can waste money—and make problems worse. In 2012, a school system in Huntsville, Alabama, adopted a one-to-one laptop and iPad program and a digital textbook curriculum. But the technology conversion actually made everyday tasks more difficult for students and teachers. Because the system lacked the necessary bandwidth to support the new machinery, one seventh-grader explained, "The websites that the books are on take forever to load and sometimes kick you out of the program. What used to be 10-minute homework is now two-hour homework." One parent of a sixth-grader lamented that the digital curriculum could only be accessed on the Internet, saying, "We drive nearly 25 minutes one way to soccer practice at least two times per week. That is two hours that she could have been doing homework, but instead, now, with textbooks only online, that is not possible." Another parent termed the initiative a "negligent disaster at best."[4]

The takeaway here is simple. If you could download a "better" operating system for your smartphone but you knew it would restrict your coverage, wipe out important contacts, or reduce battery life, you might choose to stay with your "outdated" system. The same holds when it comes to education technology. Devices, software, and the rest are helpful only if they solve problems without introducing new, bigger ones. This advice seems pretty obvious, but you'd be surprised (well, perhaps you wouldn't) how often it gets ignored.

Bryan Goodwin, chief operating officer at Mid-continent Research for Education and Learning, echoes this point, "Rather than being a cure-all or silver bullet, one-to-one laptop programs may simply amplify what's already occurring—for better or worse."[5] For instance, the 18,000-student Kyrene School District near Phoenix, Arizona, spent $33 million on technology and software between 2006 and 2011, or about $1,800 per student. Yet for all this, student achievement hadn't budged. Did Kyrene plan to reevaluate or change direction? Nope. It planned to spend tens of millions more over the next several years.[6]

Asked about this, Kyrene Superintendent David Schauer told the *New York Times*, "My gut is telling me we've had growth. But we have to have some measure that is valid, and we don't have that." He says, "We've jumped on bandwagons for different eras without knowing fully what we're doing. This might just be the new bandwagon. I hope not."[7] Imagine if you heard the head of internal medicine at the Massachusetts General Hospital tell the *New York Times*, "We've jumped on bandwagons . . . without knowing fully what we're doing. This [treatment] might just be the new bandwagon. I hope not." Yikes! Might make you look elsewhere for health care.

TECHNOLOGY CAN HELP WITH
THE ELEMENTS OF LEARNING

Last chapter, we ran through the key elements of a good learning environment (objectives, assessments, practice, demonstrations, information, overviews, and motivation support). How might technology help with these?

For starters, technological tools can allow us to store and share any of these elements more easily than if they were on paper. New tools can make it simpler to gather data on how students are doing, to customize their instruction, and to see what instructional approaches are or are not working.

Think how much it can help to simply store instructional resources. If educators can't readily draw on pre-existing materials, they wind up spending hours combing through their files, searching for good illustrations, or hand-crafting a baseline quiz to gauge student understanding. Even now, decades into the "computer revolution," teachers report taking anywhere from two to 10 hours per week designing their lesson plans. Freeing up even half that time would amount to perhaps two or three hours per week, giving teachers perhaps another 80 or 100 hours a year to spend diagnosing individual student needs, talking to students and families, or improving instructional technique.[8]

Technology also makes it easier for teachers to share their handiwork with colleagues. It would be crazy for every teacher to develop his or her own textbook—and no one does. The same principle can be applied across all the elements of learning. For example, when one of us taught high school social studies in the early 1990s, he invested enormous time and energy in developing elaborate simulations (if you're curious, a set of these was later published as the book *Bringing the Social Sciences Alive*[9]). But each of those simulations required 20 hours or more to develop, so devising five or six a year translated to 100 hours or more that couldn't be spent tutoring, mentoring, or responding to written work. Moreover, a single teacher hand-tooling everything inevitably required compromises when it came to quality.

Back then, sharing materials with departmental colleagues required lugging around boxes of instructional materials. Sharing that work with colleagues at other schools, much less those in other districts or states, was just not practical. Now compare that experience with contemporary online ventures that allow teachers to share instructional units, materials, and lesson plans. Technology can help make exemplary materials widely and freely available.

For instance, Washington, DC-based LearnZillion has built much of its strategy around what cofounder Eric Westendorf terms the "Sunday night problem." Westendorf says, "A common problem is that a teacher has to teach a lesson in the morning and it's something that they've never taught before or that they don't know how to teach that well. What do they do? Usually, they scramble to read up on it, e-mail friends for lesson plans, start searching online, and stay up late trying to throw something together. The thing is, there are a lot of great teachers out there who've already designed great lesson plans and put together high-quality instructional materials. We can even identify some of those teachers based on student performance."

So, LearnZillion has issued "casting calls" to identify terrific teachers who can demonstrate success at helping students master particular math and science objectives. LearnZillion then brings this "dream team" together, to craft, share, polish, and capture brief instructional units and the associated learning materials. Each unit features audio of the teacher providing instruction, accompanying video, instructional materials, and a "director's cut" of the instructor explaining what they're doing. The technology enables any classroom teacher to easily modify the materials (for instance, by using an app that reproduces the materials in the teacher's own handwriting), and the units include a script so that instructors can readily rerecord the instruction in their own voice.

Does LearnZillion "replace" teachers? Of course not. Wasn't it always possible for teachers to share lesson plans, borrow resources from accomplished teachers, or modify a colleagues' materials? Yep. But LearnZillion has made each of these things more affordable, reliable, available, customizable, and data-rich.

What about the rest of the elements of good instruction? As learning engineers, we tend to talk about these in the order they should be built, which is the reverse of the order they unfold instructionally—engineers start with the end goal and then work their way backwards.

Objectives

Well-constructed objectives define the skills and knowledge that students need to master in long-term memory. A focus on objectives—e.g., on competencies we care about—is a sensible way to make sure instruction, practice, and assessment tackle what matters. Part of the push to shift from a focus on "seat time" to one on "competency-based learning" is an attempt to ensure that students have the time they need to master objectives, and to allow accelerated learners to master new objectives more rapidly.

In an aligned system, objectives become the "hooks" that teachers and curriculum developers use to identify and link content. Knowing how objectives connect to each other—"What do you need to know before you can master this?"—can help organize content, assessment, and instruction.

For example, Kaplan Test Prep has looked in detail at objectives for students preparing for the MCAT exam required for admission to medical school. Many students assume, for example, that organic chemistry is the key to MCAT success. In fact, an analysis of millions of records accumulated over many years shows that physics performance is more important. Kaplan modified its instruction accordingly.

The Pittsburgh Science of Learning Center (PSLC) has rich data about objectives drawn from using computer-based "cognitive tutors" for mathematics students. When objectives are well-written there is a standard shape to the data illustrating how rapidly students master the problems. Some students solve the first problem right, an increasing number show mastery after each subsequent problem, and then the curve eventually plateaus. Sometimes, however, the data look odd; for example, the curve is too flat or bumpy, showing that students are not progressively mastering the objective. PSLC researchers have learned that by digging into the objectives in question, they can improve the instruction and accelerate student mastery (when they're successful, one result is that the learning curve becomes more "regular").

Assessments

Many teachers craft homemade assessments. One challenge is that these don't always test what they're supposed to (e.g., a math story problem may end up being about reading rather than how to multiply fractions). Nearly half of the items authored by professional test writers at places like Educational Testing Service or Pearson need to be revised or replaced because they don't "work" well when tested in the field. New technologies can make it vastly easier for teachers to check the data on assessments, to share well-constructed items and assessments, and do all this across the nation as easily as across the hall.

While complex objectives should be evaluated with appropriately complex tasks, this isn't always easy. Technology can make it easier, however, to employ "authentic" tasks. Simulation can allow instructors to have students design and run virtual experiments.[10] Good teachers and tutors can hone in on a student's mastery by asking questions close to a student's capability, saving time by skipping questions that are obviously too hard or too easy. Technology has helped make such assessments more systematic and scalable, making possible computer-adaptive tests that match the difficulty of the next question to an evolving estimate of student mastery. These adaptive assessments can cut testing time in half or less, while providing more meaningful information on student progress.[11]

Even when two students reach the same correct answer, a good flesh-and-blood tutor can see where a given student may be hesitating or backtracking. If one student stumbles his way to the right answer, it can signal that key skills or knowledge haven't been mastered in long-term memory. That student may need additional demonstrations, practice, and motivational support. Unfortunately, few schools or systems have the skilled staff needed to routinely do this kind of careful evaluation. Research suggests, however, that we can gather evidence on the pace, pattern, and confidence that students exhibit via automated assessment systems and then use that to help guide interventions.[12]

The best teachers and tutors ask a lot of questions and provide hints to help students progress. Historically, assessments lacked the agility, interactivity, or sophistication to help much on this count. Here, again, technology can help. For instance, Neil Heffernan, professor of computer science at Worcester Polytechnic Institute, and his colleagues have created the "ASSISTments" system, which shows how a hinting system within assessments can improve student learning while providing rich data to evaluate progress.[13] In a randomized controlled trial, they found a moderately large boost

(0.4 standard deviation, moving the median 50th percentile performer up to the 65th percentile) for students using the ASSISTments system instead of traditionally assigned homework.[14] In another trial, students using ASSISTments for a year of math instruction outperformed a control school. Teachers reported that increased use of the system in class resulted in more learning for the entire class, even for those students who didn't use ASSISTments (presumably because the teacher adapted instruction for all students based on the system's results).[15]

Practice

Practice is what cements learning into long-term memory. Traditionally, teachers juggling 25 or 35 students have trouble integrating lots of opportunities for practice into hectic classrooms. Textbooks and instructional materials tend to emphasize passive explanation of knowledge and concepts, partly because it's hard to craft books that offer much in the way of dynamic or authentic practice. Technology can help make it easier to provide students with opportunities to practice. Computer-assisted learning can allow a group of students to practice certain kinds of problems while teachers instruct their peers. Meanwhile, it's a lot easier for digital resources than for printed textbooks to incorporate interactive practice.

Good practice is tightly linked to good assessment. Indeed, the best practice often looks a lot like an assessment—but with a premium on explanations and feedback rather than evaluation. This is all fairly intuitive. Good swimmers get better by swimming practice laps, and they're then "evaluated" in races where they swim pretty much those same laps. Driving students practice driving and parking, and they're then evaluated in tests of how well they drive and park. Now, technology can help generate good practice tasks or items, with computer-assisted practice giving learners more opportunities to practice at their own pace. In a classroom setting, time-strapped teachers charged with serving an array of students often feel pressed to move on after a fixed amount of time—especially if most of the class is growing restless while only a few students need more practice and feedback. One-on-one tutoring can help, but that's a pricey option—even when it's available. Technology offers a promising alternative.

Kaplan Test Prep is experimenting with an adaptive home-work engine for SAT test prep that adjusts the level of practice based upon a student's progress. This adjustment helps ensure that a student's working memory is not overwhelmed while pre-paring for class. The engine also suggests how the instructor can break the class into three different group activities related to a given topic, based on student performance. Now we know you're thinking, "Wait a minute, that's nothing that a good teacher doesn't do every day as part of sensible diagnosis and differentia-tion." Exactly. Remember, technology rarely allows us to do things that are wholly *new*. Instead, it makes it easier to do these things, and lets all instructors do them more reliably.

Technology can help boost the motivation and personaliza-tion of practice by matching drills, items, and exercises to student interests and goals. Writing prompts can draw on information about student interests to better match the student with a subject she'll find interesting. This can increase the likelihood that the student will be engaged and take the practice seriously. Again, there's nothing here that creative, hardworking teachers can't do; it's just that the technology makes it more routine and less exhausting. Moreover, computer-assisted practice can more read-ily encompass banks of essay-writing topics, making things easier for teachers who may not be personally expert in everything that engages their students.

Technology can also make it possible, for instance, to instantly share essays with coaches or respondents across the globe. Remote instructors can provide additional feedback and coaching. Such support can reduce the burden on teachers and perhaps incline them to assign more real writing tasks. Computerized practice items can provide rich data about student learning, enabling teachers to provide additional, customized practice time. This whole process is not that far off from what high-end games like *World of Warcraft* are doing when they mod-ify challenges and customize difficulty level based on player behavior.[16]

Indeed, there's a lot of discussion about the value of the "gami-fication" of learning practice. Well-designed computer games are so engrossing because they provide copious practice while activating our learning machinery in the right way. They succeed because of the "learnification" of gaming.[17] Challenging, popular games suggest that, when tasks are challenging but doable, learning can be fun. One first-grader told the eminent learning psychologist Seymour Papert, after struggling with a computer programming task, that the experience was "hard fun." This is a description that aptly characterizes the best games and the best learning.[18]

Demonstrations and Information

Demonstrations and information give students conceptual knowledge and examples of what a task looks like when done well. While the best teachers are terrific at demonstrating and providing essential information, there is enormous variability across classrooms. Technology can provide consistent access to well-designed demonstrations that effectively combine audio, text, and visuals. Adding informal, targeted voice-overs to well-designed videos makes a real difference, and more promising developments are on the horizon. A research group at the University of Maastricht experimented with video and voice-overs to train pediatricians. They found that adding circles to the video to highlight areas of interest on an infant helped, but that blurring details outside the area of visual interest worked even better—presumably because the blurring permitted working memory to avoid having to process extraneous information.[19]

Tutor.com is a commercially available service that provides live, 24/7, one-on-one tutoring for students in a raft of subjects. Rather than requiring students to wait until the next day to get an explanation of a confusing concept or to see a demonstration of a problem-solving strategy, students can go online and get an immediate response from an experienced instructor. This kind of anytime, anywhere support is something that elite boarding schools with residential tutors have long been able to provide, but that has historically been impractical for most schools and families.

Interactive technologies can begin to blur the distinction between demonstrations, information, and practice, while making it easier to provide more structured demonstrations for students with less background (to avoid overloading working memory) and briefer demonstrations for students who are about ready to engage in practice.

Overviews

Overviews help learners know how the next piece fits with what they've done and what they're going to do. Describing the activities to come creates clarity and explains why the topic is relevant. This reduces potential drag on working memory and can help boost motivation. Overviews with technology-delivered media can illustrate the importance of the objectives for a student's own career or interests, show interviews with experts, depict samples of work, and more. There's an opportunity here to more effectively and reliably combat motivation problems, especially to make the case that what's being learned is important or relevant to their goals.

As with demonstrations and information, technology-delivered overviews don't have to be passive: Questions can be asked and decisions looked for, and learners likely gain from such engagement. Sophisticated data can make it possible to customize overviews for different learners, depending on their background, interests, and personal goals.

Motivation Support

Technology can help support motivation in various ways. For instance, a virtual experience—such as a simulation depicting the impact of water pollution—can help students understand why an objective matters. What's more, technology-delivered motivation supports don't have to be fancy. Even simple efforts to engage students and to focus them on learning can make a big difference.

In one notable study, several hundred students took a four-hour online Microsoft Excel training course. After each one-hour module, some students were asked questions about how they were learning the material. The researchers found that the questions increased student retention markedly. The questions weren't all that dazzling; they consisted only of simple text prompts like, "Have I spent enough time reviewing to remember the information after I finish the course?" or, "Am I focusing my mental effort on the training material?" Nonetheless, the impact on learning was substantial. The performance of students given the prompts improved by 5% on a 15-item multiple-choice measure that included both factual information (such as "which dialog box do you use to write an If function?") and procedural knowledge (such as "you have already done . . . and now want to do . . . what is your next step?").[20]

Technology can make it easier to record ongoing diagnostic information allowing supports to be targeted. Are students spending less time than expected on a learning activity? Are their assignments getting turned in late? Direct questions about students' engagement can help complete the picture, too. Once a problem is identified, students get either teacher-mediated or technology-mediated support.

University of Wisconsin-Milwaukee professors have used an approach called Amplified Assistance to target students who need feedback. Instructors use the school's learning management system to identify students who might be struggling and then use model e-mail templates to provide constructive, proactive assistance. The indicators and feedback are designed to address both motivation and content troubles. These resources make it less likely that faculty will wait until students reach out to them, and more likely they will lend a hand before students get too lost. The templates speed up feedback, offer guidance to faculty who are uncertain of what to say, and make it feasible to communicate with an entire class in the same time it once took to address a handful of students. In an initial controlled trial with more than 1,700 students, the results were promising: The share of students getting an "A" or a "B" for the course in question increased by about 16 percentage points—or roughly 100%![21]

PUTTING PEOPLE AND TECHNOLOGY TOGETHER

Technology allows people to work better and smarter. It allows them to do more of what they do best—while providing a cheaper, easier way to tackle routine tasks or to provide learning support that teachers can't provide.

Take the unsexy, low-tech challenge of improving writing, about which there is an established body of learning science.[22] One demonstrably effective technique is the one we've talked about before, having students write syntheses of good essays they read.

Is this a promising avenue from a learning engineer's standpoint? First, there's high-quality research suggesting it works (usually a good sign). Second, the intuition is consistent with two principles from learning science: Learners need a lot of deliberate practice to get good at things, and they benefit from "worked examples" of complex tasks, where they do some of the hard work and some of it is already done for them. In this case, a previously written, quality essay is a kind of worked example, with much of the research already done for the student. Extracting the argument and key points from the essay and writing those up briefly becomes a manageable, scaffolded project.

Note that this learning technique requires no technology at all. However, rather than stopping there, ask: How can technology help make this more affordable, reliable, available, customizable, and data-rich? For starters, a key problem with writing assignments is the markup and grading process. When instructors are marking papers by hand, it takes too long to get students good feedback rapidly enough for them to rewrite many pieces.

How can technology help? Consider online mediated essay grading services, like those provided by SmartThinking, Inc., an online tutoring service. It's still in the early stages, but even now it can take a block of essays turned in by students and get reader comments back within 24 hours. That lets teachers and students quickly move on to deliberate practice. This can be very exciting for a learning engineer if it can operate under existing constraints on pricing, technology available, and so forth.

There are also services (e.g., the Educational Testing Service's Criterion service, or Vantage Learning's Intellimetric system[23]) that provide *automated* essay grading. Automated essay-grading systems spit back a grade plus minor feedback on grammar and spelling. Even if that grade matches how a good teacher would mark the essay, the systems aren't providing the kind of feedback students can dig their teeth into. Now, if the problem is grading large numbers of papers and providing routine feedback, these solutions can be great. However, if the problem is finding a way to give students richer feedback and generate more practice writing based on that feedback, these solutions don't help as much.

There may be additional automated essay marking and grading systems that are better suited to solve the essay practice problem. One of them might be SAGrader, which uses a completely different method for generating grades and content comments for an essay, and might work well for the synthesis exercise we're talking about. It requires someone, like the teacher or curriculum developer, to install a structured version of the content to be covered in the student paper, and then, using fancy computer techniques such as "fuzzy logic," look for those concepts and terms in a linked structure within the student's writing. It not only provides overall scores, it also offers comments that students may find helpful.

What do these look like? For an example, take an assignment in which "students were asked to (among other things) read a hypothetical life history, identify six concepts related to social stratification, and define each concept."[24] The computer feedback listed the correctly identified concepts, noting that the student received partial credit for including most of the six, while indicating that there were still more to identify.

Let's be clear—no one, especially us, thinks that this counts as incisive feedback. But it doesn't have to be, so long as it's useful and allows teachers to focus on something more important than checking whether each student had covered each of the required items. The benefit here, as the folks at SAGrader note, is not just the substantive feedback and the speed with which it's generated, but that the instant feedback seems to increase students' appetite to rewrite. A pilot in which 172 students penned more than 1,100 essays in an introductory sociology course found that students revised 71% of the assignments based on SAGrader feedback. (Anyone who has ever taught high school or college would regard that alone as a pretty heartening state of affairs.) Essays that were not revised by students averaged a score of 87 out of 100. Meanwhile, essays revised by students started with an average score of 61 and ended with an average score of 91.[25] In other words, the students who were struggling most seemed to put in the time and effort needed to boost their performance until it exceeded that of their peers.

Technology can free teachers from having to provide some or all of the "broadcast" work, elements like overviews, information, and demonstrations. This allows them to focus their time on coaching, questioning, providing feedback to practice, motivating, and personalizing students' experience. (We'll talk more about this in the context of "flipped" classrooms in Chapter 4.)

PUTTING THIS TO WORK

Today, technology allows a teacher in Seattle to teach students in Syracuse. This entails a certain remove between teacher and student, but also makes it much easier to match students to teachers on the basis of expertise, interest, or style. Social media can enable teachers to connect with colleagues interested in the same topics, students, or challenges. With well-designed assessment tools, groups of geographically dispersed teachers can discuss results and collaborate on new practices in ways that were once simply not feasible. Researchers, developers, and teachers of various grade levels can now cross-pollinate new ideas, sharing what's known about learning, what evidence is accumulating, and how new technologies can matter.

In other words, we've seen the emergence of a wealth of new instructional possibilities. Yet those new capabilities can be used poorly or not at all. To be helpful, a new technology ought to offer discernible benefits somewhere within a learning framework of objectives, assessments, practice, demonstrations, information, overview, and support for motivation. If you can't figure out where, exactly, it makes a difference, then be wary.

Taking full advantage of technology to enhance the learning process requires a willingness to look at proposed solutions and ask tough questions. Next chapter, we'll start to explore how this kind of thinking applies when it comes to school redesign.

NOTES

1. VanLehn, K. (2011). The Relative Effectiveness of Human Tutoring, Intelligent Tutoring Systems,and Other Tutoring Systems. *Educational Psychologist, 46*(4), 197-221.
2. Blueprint Schools Network. (2012). Blueprint Apollo 20 Fellows Program: Frequently asked questions. Retrieved from http://apollo20fellows.org/
3. Houston Independent School District. (2012). Facts and figures about HISD. Retrieved from http://www.houstonisd.org/
4. Bonvlillian, C. (2012, September 16). Glitches in schools' digital initiative have Huntsville parents, teachers frustrated. *The Huntsville Times*. [Web log post]. Posted on http://blog.al.com/breaking /2012/09/glitches_in_schools_digital_in.html

5. Richtel, M. (2011, September 3). In classroom of future, stagnant scores. *New York Times*. Retrieved from http://www.nytimes.com

6. Richtel, M. (2011, September 3). In classroom of future, stagnant scores. *New York Times*. Retrieved from http://www.nytimes.com

7. Richtel, M. (2011, September 3). In classroom of future, stagnant scores. *New York Times*. Retrieved from http://www.nytimes.com

8. Based on reports from the ProTeacher website. Retrieved from http://www.proteacher.net

9. See Hess, F.M. (1999). *Bringing the social sciences alive: 10 simulations for history, economics, government, and geography.* Needham Heights, MA: Allyn & Bacon.

10. Triona, L. M., & Klahr, D. (2003). Point and click or grab and heft: Comparing the influence of physical and virtual instructional materials on elementary school students' ability to design experiments. Department of Psychology. Carnegie Mellon University. Paper 336. Retrieved from http://repository.cmu.edu/psychology/336

11. Linn, R. L. (Ed.). (1989). *Educational measurement* (3rd edition). Madison, WI: National Council on Measurement in Education, p. 385.

12. Paul, A. M. (2012, September 12). The machines are taking over. *New York Times*. Retrieved from http://www.nytimes.com

13. Heffernan, N. T., & Koedinger, K. R. (2012). *Integrating assessment within instruction: A look forward.* Paper presented at the Invitational research symposium on technology enhanced assessments, Education Testing Service, May 7–8, 2012.

14. Mendicino, M., Razzaq, L., & Heffernan, N. T. (2009). Comparison of traditional homework with computer supported homework. *Journal of Research on Technology in Education, 41*(3), 331–359.

15. Koedinger, K. R., McLaughlin, E., & Heffernan, N. (2010). A quasi-experimental evaluation of an on-line formative assessment and tutoring system. *Journal of Educational Computing Research, 43*(1), 489–510.

16. Gee, J. P. (2003). *What video games have to teach us about learning and literacy.* New York, NY: Palgrave/Macmillan.

17. Gee, J. P. (2003). *What video games have to teach us about learning and literacy.* New York, NY: Palgrave Macmillan.

18. Papert, S. (2002). Hard fun. *Bangor Daily News*. Retrieved from http://papert.org/articles/HardFun.html

19. Jarodzka, H., Balsley, T., Holmqvist, K., Nystrom, M., Scheiter, K., Gerjets, P., & Eika, B. (2012). Conveying clinical reasoning based on visual observation via eye-movement modeling examples. *Instructional Science, 40*, 813–827.

20. Sitzmann, T., & Ely, K. (2010). Sometimes you need a reminder: The effects of prompting self-regulation on regulatory processes, learning, and attrition. *Journal of Applied Psychology, 95*(1), 132–144.

21. Reddy, D. M., et al. (2011). U-Pace: Facilitating academic success for all students. *EDUCAUSE Quarterly, 34*(4), n4.

22. Graham, S., & Perin, D. (2007). *Writing next: Effective strategies to improve writing of adolescents in middle and high schools.* A report to Carnegie Corporation of New York. Washington, DC: Alliance for Excellent Education.

23. To learn more about Educational Testing Service's Criterion service visit http://criterion.ets.org; to learn more about Vantage Learning's IntelliMetric system, visit http://www.vantagelearning.com/products/intellimetric

24. Brent, E., Atkisson, C., Green, N. (2009). Time-shifted online collaboration: Creating teachable moments through automated grading. In A. A. Juan, T. Daradournis, & S. Caballe (Eds.), *Monitoring and assessment in online collaborative environments: Emergent computational technologies for e-learning support,* pp. 55–74. Hershey, PA: Information Science Reference.

25. Jarodzka, H., Balsley, T., Holmqvist, K., Nystrom, M., Scheiter, K., Gerjets, P., & Eika, B. (2012). Conveying clinical reasoning based on visual observation via eye-movement modeling examples. *Instructional Science, 40,* 813–827.

CHAPTER 4

Reengineering With Technology

T echnology can be a powerful lever for rethinking schools and systems. But it's the rethinking that should occupy the spotlight. As education leadership authority Michael Fullan has noted, "There is no evidence that technology is a particularly good entry point for whole system reform."[1] Technology can provide tools to help deliver knowledge, support students, extend and deepen instruction, and refashion cost structures. Unfortunately, too many educators, industry figures, and technology enthusiasts seem to imagine that technology itself will be a difference-maker.

Jared Covili, a professional development trainer in Utah who helps schools integrate technology, sees many schools buy technology without a strategy for use. The result: Nothing really changes. He says, "A school might run out and buy 200 iPads before they really have a strategy. If you don't have a vision for what you want to do in your own building, iPads really kind of become just a device to check e-mail and maybe play some games on. Instead of showing your PowerPoint through a projector off of your computer, now you're using your iPad to do it. . . . [I]t hasn't really changed the instruction. It's just changed the way you're presenting it." As *Disrupting Class* coauthor Michael Horn notes, "The education system's inclination when it sees a potentially disruptive technology is to cram it into its existing model to sustain what it is already doing."[2]

Enthusiasm for wildly new "disruptive innovation" has sometimes blinded us to the fact that, 90% of the time, technology's biggest impact is optimizing or enhancing familiar tasks and routines. This frees up time, talent, and dollars for better uses, fueling improvement. If teachers with one-to-one devices can, each day, spend 10 minutes fewer entering data, 10 minutes fewer passing out and collecting texts and papers, and five minutes fewer pulling up student assessment results when working to differentiate instruction, they can save more than two hours a week—or more than 70 hours a year! That's time they can devote to instruction, mentoring, or lesson design. That's a giant benefit, and likely to be more significant than from learning solutions that are touted as more revolutionary.

Too often, rather than using new tools to free up time or make better use of talent or resources, new solutions are ladled over what's already in place. Steve Hockett, principal of Colvin Run Elementary in Fairfax County, Virginia, and former principal in residence at the U.S. Department of Education, says, "I've gone into schools where they say, 'We have smart, interactive white-boards in every classroom.' And then I'll go visit classrooms and they're basically using the whiteboard as an overhead projector where the print can't even be seen in the back of the room. So it's not interactive and it's not even a very good overhead projector, yet it costs $2,500. . . . If I were to say, 'What am I seeing that's not successful?' it's people who are basically spending lots of money to own a Ferrari to drive a block to the store and back every day."

Hockett faced a familiar problem. He explains, "Our schools have immersion programs that kids can opt to go to where they learn math, social studies, and science in a second language. For instance, in second grade, a school might get half of their instruc-tion in a subject in Spanish. Our school tried to participate in the program twice, but we didn't get it, and then the funding all went out because of the budget. We needed an alternative to a fully funded program with new staff. So I was talking to the PTO [par-ent-teacher organization] president about it and I said, 'I wonder why we just don't do Rosetta Stone or something and teach our kids Spanish.' So we looked into it and we did it, starting with first and second grade."

The challenge: Hockett quickly realized that simply adopting Rosetta Stone as a stand-alone wasn't going to work. He explains, "At that point, Rosetta Stone was just for the student. So it was totally asynchronous. Our first- and second-graders were bored to tears. So the intent was good but the implementation and practice weren't that successful. It wasn't as engaging for kids. . . . We put our heads together, and we decided that we love the idea of kids getting Spanish instruction, but we had to change how we're delivering it. So, with additional PTO support, we decided to have first- and second-graders get Spanish twice a week with a Spanish teacher. For Grades 3 through 6, 50% of their time was spent with Rosetta Stone and 50% with a teacher." Colvin Run used new technologies to enrich learning in ways that fit its constraints. Hockett identified a strategy for using those tools, determined what was and wasn't working, and then made sensible modifica-tions. This is how a learning engineer operates.

How can we be sure to get this right? For a clue, think back to our discussion of your familiar, friendly book in Chapter 1, and how it successfully yielded transformational change in teaching and learning. Indeed, there are other familiar learning "technologies" that have had big impacts—so familiar, we don't think of them as technologies at all.

THE SOCRATIC METHOD

Consider a "learning technology" that's even older than the book: the "Socratic method." The Socratic method is the most basic approach imaginable to assessing, diagnosing, and intervening with students. Compared to the lecture, with its emphasis on conveying information, the Socratic method is a basic "technology" for helping to cultivate mastery through practice and feedback. Why was Socrates so skeptical of the written word? Because it threatened to undermine the genius of the instructional approach that now bears his name.

In the Socratic method, the teacher challenges students with questions that stimulate the application of new information, provide feedback, build critical thinking, upend comfortable assumptions, and illuminate ideas. It's a dialectical method, in which the teacher often plays devil's advocate, pitting herself against whatever response the student provides. The technique is often used to lead the student to contradict himself in some way, in order to steer him toward a new understanding or insight.

Where books are fixed, the Socratic method is dynamic. Where books must be pitched at some median reader, the Socratic method permits constant adjustment to the interests, limitations, and needs of a given student. In the hands of a skilled instructor, the Socratic method is perhaps the most powerful model we have for promoting understanding, engagement, and mastery through individualized practice and feedback.

So if we already have such a powerful tool to encourage learning, why can't we use it to improve learning at scale?

The problem is twofold. First, the Socratic method is really hard to do well. Lots of people might try to do it or might think they're doing it, only to execute it poorly. Second, the Socratic method is really expensive. Employing this method of teaching requires a skilled educator working with a class of perhaps

15 students. Thus, it's really difficult to effectively deliver the Socratic method at scale.

This is where a learning engineer asks whether technology might help extend the benefits of the Socratic method, just as the book made available at scale, at least in part, the benefits of the best teachers. Maybe we can't clone the best Socratic teachers, but perhaps we can duplicate some of the benefits they provide and deliver those to a broad population.

This is exactly the way to think about those intelligent tutoring systems from Chapter 3. The question is not whether such systems can match the best human tutors but whether they can provide millions of students a tutoring experience that's affordable, accessible, and "good enough" to support learning.

THE ENCYCLOPEDIA

A familiar piece of learning technology is that increasingly outdated standby, the encyclopedia. The encyclopedia uses book technology to make knowledge of a wide array of phenomena and facts universally available. In truth, once upon a time, the encyclopedia was massively successful at doing this. Encyclopedias first reached a mass audience in the 1920s, when multivolume sets like *World Book, Encyclopaedia Britannica,* and *Collier's* were sold door to door. These volumes made a wealth of information suddenly available in an accessible fashion. They were also vast, unwieldy, and incredibly expensive, selling, by the 1980s, for between $500 and $2,000 a set.[3] Sales of *Britannica* peaked in 1990, when it grossed $650 million.[4]

Encyclopedias provided a unique, valuable resource. Indeed, it was once considered a parental failing for a family with a sufficient income to not invest in an encyclopedia. But the cost, unwieldiness, and inability to update an existing set were all big limitations. New information technology led designers to ask how they might provide this vast body of information without asking readers to fumble through reams of paper and dizzying amounts of text, in a more user-friendly and affordable fashion.

Born in the mid-1980s as a brainchild of Bill Gates, Encarta was Microsoft's response to that question. Microsoft released the $99 CD-ROM software in 1993 and sold more than a million copies the following year.[5] Eventually available online and on DVD, the complete English version of Encarta contained 62,000 authored articles at its peak—or 50% more entries than the most comprehensive version of the *Encyclopaedia Britannica*.[6]

But Encarta had its own limitations. It was self-contained, couldn't be updated in real time, and was expensive to produce, and accessing it required sitting at a computer. As the web and then smartphones became more widely available, Encarta rapidly grew obsolete. It finally faded away in 2009, giving way to the crowd-sourced, more collaborative (and free) online encyclopedia Wikipedia. Launched in 2001, Wikipedia contains over 4 million English articles—or about 100 times as many entries as the most comprehensive version of the *Encyclopaedia Britannica*. When it discontinued Encarta, Microsoft explained, "The category of traditional encyclopedias and reference material has changed. . . . People today seek and consume information in considerably different ways than in years past."[7] That's exactly right. The encyclopedia was a better way to share a vast quantity of accumulated human knowledge than simple memorization. And free online collections that are continuously curated with a hundred times as much information are a better way yet.

NEW TOOLS *CAN* CREATE NEW CAPABILITIES

If we view technology as a tool, a couple of things become clear. First, using technology in the classroom is nothing new. We've always used tools to support learning, whether those were the Socratic method, book, pencil, film projector, or calculator. Like the tools that came before, today's learning technologies are often just cheaper, faster, more universal ways to do things we've always done. As Idaho state superintendent Tom Luna has said, "Technology is not replacing teachers . . . technology is replacing chalk."[8] There are cases, however, where they can also offer the opportunity to do things that were previously impractical.

For example, for all the recent enthusiasm over virtual schooling, distance learning isn't a new idea. In the United States, distance learning can be traced back at least to the correspondence courses of the 1800s. In that sense, online instruction is just a faster, better, more accessible way to deliver that instruction.

Contemporary technology makes possible remote interaction between teacher and student that's dynamic, interactive, and customizable in a way that was once inconceivable.

Consider how the emergence of new capabilities plays out in the case of two familiar challenges: teacher evaluation and extended learning time.

Boosting the Value of Teacher Observation

With all of the attention that states and districts are according to teacher evaluation, a persistent challenge is finding ways to create more time for helpful and rigorous observation. The problem? Just think about the mechanics of teacher observation. An observer may sit in the back of a classroom for 30 or 40 minutes, recording what she observes by hand. After class (if the teacher has a break) or when there's an opportunity, the observer and teacher will discuss the class, with the observer discussing from her notes and the teacher trying to recall what happened. The whole exercise may require an hour or more of observer time, as well as the need for the observer to travel for the class and then hang around until she and the teacher can connect.

Consider how a 21st century professional baseball coach might handle the same situation. If he's watching a player take swings in the batting cage, the coach might have the player stop each time there's something worth noting—addressing it in real time. More likely, though, the coach won't stand there and watch each player take each swing; after all, that's time-consuming and logistically difficult. And, practically speaking, it's impossible for a coach to give that player real-time feedback when he's in the batter's box during games. So, what does the coach do? He tapes all of a player's swings—in games or practices—and then reviews those with the player when it's most useful.

Los Angeles Angels first baseman Albert Pujols, a perennial all-star, has casually noted that he travels everywhere with a laptop that includes video of every single swing he's taken in the past decade. That way, the coach needn't try to describe what he saw; the coach and the player are watching the same thing simultaneously, and it can be slowed down and repeated, and compared to prior efforts to fix a flaw. It makes for a more concrete and useful session—and something the player and the coach can revisit, as needed.

Bringing that same intuition to teacher evaluation makes two things possible. The first is using technology to do teacher observation and evaluation more effectively and efficiently. The second is leveraging technology to think in wholly new ways about these tasks.

Start with the first, more modest, goal. A school with 40 teachers, each needing to be observed at least five times a year, requires a minimum of 200 observations across the school year. If each observation requires an observer sitting in the back of the classroom, with that observer arranging to meet with the teacher as soon as is feasible after class, that probably adds up to 200 hours or more of observation, feedback, and reporting time. During the bulk of that time, the observer isn't working *with* the teacher and providing feedback, but is instead taking notes, waiting to meet with the teacher, or filling out forms. Even during the actual feedback session, the teacher can't see what was or wasn't happening in the classroom—he can only listen to the observer and try to recall what was happening inside the class and inside his head at the time.

Technology offers the chance to reengineer this process. Imagine the school possesses even a couple of digital classroom cameras (at the high end, similar to panoramic cameras supplied by companies like Teachscape, but they don't have to be this fancy). This changes the observer process: The teacher can record his own class, independent of an observer's schedule or travel. They can schedule a debrief at a mutually convenient time, confident that they won't forget what happened in the class (at least, the events outside the teacher's head—to get the teacher's perspective on what he was thinking, they still wouldn't want to wait too long). The observer can watch the tape ahead of time, perhaps even make notes online, rubric in hand, using a video discussion tool like Vialogue. The observer saves time, logistical challenges are reduced, and the feedback session becomes much more dynamic and specific. If both teacher and observer make notes during their discussion, there's a very specific artifact that both can review later.

If a school stretches a little more, the technology makes it possible to rethink the entire process of structured observation. Cameras and video make it possible for a teacher who thinks, "Hey, I'd like some coaching or feedback on this lesson—it's always a tough one," to get it, even when no designated observer is available. That teacher can tape the lesson and then arrange to watch it on a laptop at a bar later that afternoon with a colleague or two, brainstorming what to do next time, or with the assistant principal before school the following day—or even to share it virtually with a mentor somewhere else in the world while holding a Skyped conversation about what they're seeing.

Suddenly, new career opportunities open up for teacher coaches. Why not a sideline as the city's best fourth-grade "fractions misconceptions" lesson coach? Or what about building a portfolio of coaching topics, put out a virtual shingle that says "The coach is in!" and charge $40 an hour for mentoring? Why not become the best fraction misconceptions lesson coach in the western United States, for students aged about 10–14, then link up with other coaches with complementary skills? And then tape your own coaching sessions with teachers so that you can find a mentor who can coach *you* on how you're working with your colleagues.

In other words, technology makes it newly possible to have the kind of engaged, sustained coaching that's so difficult to provide when it depends on individuals traveling to view classrooms, when a debrief has to happen almost immediately to be useful, when opportunities for feedback are constrained by scheduling, and when communication and coaching delivery are restricted by physical presence and time. And, by the way, it creates terrific new opportunities for professional educators to grow and share their skills.

Making Homework More Useful

Students are in class for about six hours a day, 180 days a year. For many students, that's clearly not enough time to learn all that we might wish. So, we ask students to read textbooks at home and to solve problems, write papers, and tackle projects as homework. The problem: Students often don't do the reading and assignments, might need more explanation, or may do the work halfheartedly and in isolation.

Worse, most textbooks are mediocre from a learning science standpoint—they're too distracting, pay insufficient heed to how words and illustrations work together, and use language that's frequently too difficult for tough topics. Pitched at a mythical median student, textbooks also inevitably are not suited to the optimal level for the majority of students. What's more, even if a student does the assignment, the potential benefit is lost if the teacher simply lectures on the same material the next day in class and doesn't engage students in practice and feedback concerning what they read.

One promising response to this dilemma is the emergence of the "flipped classroom" model popularized by schools and systems taking advantage of video lessons from Khan Academy. (For those unfamiliar with the term "flipped classroom," it typically means that schools have "flipped" the instructional model by asking students to view taped lectures as homework, so that they can engage in collaborative, active learning during class, including the problem solving that used to be the homework.)

Now, in theory, books were also an attempt to "flip" the classroom. As we noted in Chapter 1, the book made it possible to learn at home things that students could previously learn only in school. However, in practice the book has often disappointed. We can flip the classroom, but let's think carefully about what's changed. The video lessons may be good, or mediocre, from a learning science standpoint. Students may not watch the assignment. Even if they do watch, the teacher will defeat the purpose if he just reviews the content the next day in class.

It may be that online lessons can be more engaging and appealing for 21st century students, but it seems many of the familiar challenges remain, including one of the biggest: What does a teacher do if five students out of 30 don't do the assignment the night before? Whether the teacher is using books or videos, there's a high chance that those five students are the ones who are faring most poorly, and teachers feel obliged to spend a lot of class time focused on reteaching or reviewing the lesson with an eye to those students, potentially limiting the practice-and-feedback benefit from the flipped structure.

Breaking that dynamic is not a question of having the technology but of how teachers use it. Successful designs start with identifying the problem. One problem may be that the assigned work, whether video- or text-based, isn't a good fit for a student's current level of mastery (e.g., what that student has in long-term memory). One-to-one tutoring could solve this, of course, but that can be tough to manage. Now the proper learning engineering question becomes, "Can technology help solve this in a better way?"

Imagine that the learning system used information about baseline student mastery to decide what video and practice to provide a student *this* evening. The suggestions could be based on the experiences of hundreds or thousands of other students who are "like" this student in important ways. The system could then provide a learning experience that draws on what this student has already mastered, and that—because it's challenging but not too challenging—may be more likely to motivate the student.

Let's take this a little further: Imagine that after the homework is completed, the system provides information and guidance to the teacher about the next day's instruction. It suggests which students should engage in which activities, based on their interests and level of mastery. This makes it exceptionally easy for the teacher to differentiate instruction.

Does this sound too far-fetched? Too impractical? Guess again. Aside from the use of video, this describes the SmartTrack system, mentioned in Chapter 3 and used by Kaplan in many of its SAT test-preparation environments. Before an in-class session, students work with an adaptive learning system that allows them to work on practice problems that match their level of mastery. The system then makes recommendations as to which students should be assigned to which subgroups for specific additional activities in the class.

So this can be done. Should *you* do it? Can you do it well? Those are the questions that preoccupy a learning engineer.

ENGINEERS ASK A LOT OF QUESTIONS

Engineers start by asking a lot of questions. Why? If you build stuff without asking a lot of questions about who'll be using it, how they'll be using it, and why they'll be using it, you make it a lot less likely that you'll engineer anything very useful. Asking questions like this is how engineers make sure they know what problem they're solving.

Patrick Larkin, assistant superintendent in Burlington, Massachusetts, who led a one-to-one iPad adoption when he was principal of Burlington High School, offers an example of how to do this right: "It's not about the technology; we're not training teachers to say 'How do I use the iPad in my classroom?' I think the questions we got better at asking were, 'What are my goals that I'm trying to accomplish with my students? What are the learning outcomes that I'm looking for?' That's always the first question whether you're in an environment that has technology or not. And with the support of some of our integration specialists, they're able to come in and help show ways teachers can get to those benchmarks faster or get more assessment data."

Dennis Villano is one of those specialists; he oversees technology integration for Burlington Public Schools. He sees his job as one that focuses on the learning process first and products second: "It's something I really feel very strongly about. I think that schools need to flip their way of thinking, and they've got to stop thinking about applications first, and then devices, and then infrastructure last—they need to think about why they're doing it. They need to let the educators drive technology and not necessarily let the IT departments be the driving factor. We've kind of flipped the way that we've traditionally thought about educational technology and we've gone for why it's important, not so much what's the coolest new toy that's out there and available to buy."

This kind of focus is essential. It points to the right questions. What's not working with how the problem is currently being addressed? What needs to be done differently? Do students need more powerful instruction, time-on-task, remediation, or high-quality assessment and feedback? Do faculties need more support, better data, or coaching? In any of these cases, how might technological tools help?

The tendency of technology enthusiasts to overpromise and of skeptics to insist that new technology will undermine schooling suffer from the same confusion. What matters is not the technology, but what it can do to promote learning. The place to start when it comes to technology is *not by focusing on the technology but on the learning challenge.*

Readers may note the similarities to the concept of "design thinking" that we've mentioned before. In K–12 circles, "design thinking" is sometimes understood to mean having students solve complex design problems.[9] We have something different in mind. Tim Brown, CEO and president of IDEO, an international design firm, for instance, notes that we often believe "Great ideas pop fully formed out of brilliant minds, in feats of imagination well beyond the abilities of mere mortals." The truth, he reminds us, is that design is a process of hard work, creative discovery, and "iterative cycles of prototyping, testing, and refinement."[10]

Say you're fixing a house. You can note that the house is in rough shape and needs to be repaired, but that doesn't offer much guidance. It's slightly better to say the problem is that the house is leaky. But it's still not a very precise statement of the problem. Why is it leaky? Where's the water leaking in from? Is it because the roof is shot? Because there are missing windows? Because there are cracks in the foundation? Any of these problems can be addressed with the proper tools and materials, but you need to know what the actual problem is before you can fix it.

The same goes for schooling. Observing that a school is "failing" doesn't do much to help identify the problems that need solving. What is it "failing" to do? Are teachers unable to provide strong content instruction? Is there a lack of parental engagement? Do students need extra support and mentoring in particular skills or subjects? A more precise rendering of challenges and solutions can illuminate what needs to change and where technology can help. For instance, if you determine that certain students really need intensive, one-on-one tutoring, why aren't they getting it? Is it hard to find properly skilled adults locally or for your teachers to find free time to do it?

If so, you may consider exploring online tutoring. There are online tutoring providers who can provide 24/7 one-on-one tutoring in dozens of subjects. For many, the cost will work out to something less than $30 an hour.[11] In fact, community college systems pre-buy this kind of tutoring in bulk, purchasing thousands of hours at a time. If you give up one FTE and that slot costs you about $72,000 in salary and benefits (the national average), you can pick up more than 2,400 hours of one-on-one tutoring. That's an hour a week for more than 60 kids. Whether that trade-off is a good one is a matter of context, judgment, and values—a learning engineering decision.

WHAT PROBLEM IS THE IPAD SOLVING?

Schools and districts too rarely use new technologies as an opportunity to rethink their work. Instead, teachers and school leaders tend to talk excitedly about "innovation" or a single nifty lesson. Doug Levin, executive director of the State Educational Technology Directors Association (SETDA), worries about this tendency: "We do hear stories about school districts or schools that say, 'Hey, we just got a grant or we just found out we got extra money, and we're just going to go out and buy a bunch of stuff . . . and the iPad because we really like it.' And then the next question is 'What are we going to do with it?' It's a terrifying story, and I hear it unfortunately a little bit too often."[12] The result is that technologies just get overlaid on existing routines.

A learning engineer regards tablets, digital textbooks, or online learning not just as opportunities to improve instruction but also as a chance to manufacture time, extend the reach of talent, or generate savings. This starts with figuring out where you're trying to go, what problem you're trying to solve, and what barriers need to be removed in order to get there.

If we're thinking about the iPad, here are some possibilities worth considering:

- How does the iPad permit you to reconfigure professional development? Does it allow just-in-time or asynchronous training, or make it possible to customize delivery and more readily use online providers instead of drive-by, more expensive professional development?
- How much time can teachers save by taking attendance via a scanning application? In a middle school or high school, if a teacher saves three minutes a class, five times a day, they can save more than 40 instructional hours a year.
- How much can online assessment on devices speed up test taking and feedback cycles for teachers, and how should this change work routines and the dynamics of a professional learning community?
- How much time can teachers and administrators save on data entry, if the school or system is careful to ensure that it's adopting data processes that run cleanly off the tablets? If teachers are saving 20 minutes a day of data entry and record-keeping, that can add up to more than 50 hours a year of energy they can redirect into preparation or mentoring.
- Can teachers set aside pre-prepared instruction for those days when they'll be absent, or can teachers provide full classes and assignments for days when students may be sick? Given that the typical teacher misses five to 10 days a year and the typical student nearly as much, this has the potential to increase the average instructional year by 50 to 100 hours.

Such questions can help point out where tablet adoption can offer new opportunities to boost learning time, save funds, or get more value from scarce talent.

WHAT HAPPENS WHEN YOU DON'T THINK LIKE A LEARNING ENGINEER

When we confront new technologies without a learning engineering mind-set, we too often focus on the devices or the technology rather than the learning. Case in point: We were struck by the highly regarded Ohio principal (mentioned in Chapter 1), who proudly explained to us, "We encourage our students to use mobile devices. . . . For example, a couple of years ago one of our teachers allowed a student to type an entire research paper on his iPhone. It was very hard, but it was eye-opening for everybody. To us, it's like, 'How in the world did he type an entire research paper on an iPhone?' but, to him, that's the device he was comfortable with. He owned it, he used it every day, so, why not?"

Why not? Well, the iPhone is a terrific tool for a lot of things— but it's a lousy tool for writing a term paper. Sure, the student liked using it and was probably adept at doing so, but the working memory distractions of navigating and reviewing his argument a thimbleful at a time means the student couldn't readily review the organization of the writing or consider the whole of his essay. The result, in terms of helping students learn to write well, is a subpar learning experience. It's as if someone bought a private jet for a school in order to give flying lessons, and the principal decided to use it to it to plow the parking lot in winter. The school would be using sophisticated technology to do a simple task that an old pickup truck could do *better.* If the principal bragged that he was excited about his maintenance guys doing jet-based snow plowing, we hope that he'd be ridiculed, not celebrated.

When a student is doing a routine task and learning no more (or less) than before and the exercise seems noteworthy only because of the technology used, we've lost sight of what matters. We're putting the spotlight on the wrong part of the stage. We'd have been impressed if the principal had felt inclined to remark upon the *learning* or the *student's work* or something else that matters that was improved in the delivery process. He stoked our concern here when he passed right by those in his fascination with the technology itself.

Lenny Schad, former chief information officer at Katy Independent School District in Texas (now in a similar role in Houston), articulates this clearly. In discussing Katy's bring-your-own-device program, he notes that a tendency to focus on technology can lead educators and parents to talk about mobile learning and "bring your own device" initiatives as if the presence of devices inevitably improves learning. He says, "Based on what we've seen over the past three years, that couldn't be further from the truth. Mobile learning is all about changing instruction, because if the instruction inside the class doesn't change, then allowing the kids to bring their own device will do nothing. If the teacher still teaches like they did with paper and pencil, then the devices add no value. So bring your own device is not about the device; it's about an enabling tool that allows a philosophical change in instruction."

We've visited schools acclaimed for their one-to-one computing, personal computers, and iPads, only to see students scouring the web for material to cut-and-paste into a report, or desultorily dressing up rote presentations with colorful clip art and creative sound effects. This can be as true at "technology-infused" high schools as at your local elementary. Jerry Crisci, director of technology for Scarsdale Public Schools, relates, "The classic example that you see in a lot of schools is asking kids to do PowerPoint presentations where the presentation models a traditional report. If I'm studying the civil war in middle school, the assignment would be to do a PowerPoint presentation on the Civil War. They *could* flip the assignment around. For instance, you might instead ask the kids to do a presentation where you compare and contrast the attitudes of people who supported the Confederate or the Union side . . . That would entail having kids look for patterns and construct new knowledge, and not just giving a presentation on something. Which, frankly, often leads to kids just copying and pasting from a reference source."

We routinely see technology used in ways that amount to students using Google-cum-Wikipedia as a latter-day *World Book* encyclopedia. Video shorts are nice, but it's mostly us "digital tourists" who think it reflects impressive learning. Twenty years ago, even rudimentary video editing was technically challenging and required real skill. Today, it can be as simple as clicking a few buttons on iMovie. It's not a question of deep knowledge so much as a familiar set of routines. Unfortunately, it's easy for adults to get so distracted by the visuals, stylings, and sounds that we fail to note that the content is a vapid assemblage of Wikipedia-supplied factoids. Indeed, students may be distracted from taking time to synthesize and apply knowledge and procedures because, for example, they were picking the ultimate background music.

Two cautions are worth noting here. The first is that much of what passes for tech-infused learning today frequently does not mean that a student has mastered the outcomes needed for long-term success. The second is that some of what passes for "21st century skills" can involve the mastery of "skills" that actually aren't all that difficult and may even distract from the real mastery needed for the long haul.

Terms like "digital natives" can be unhelpful when they suggest that any skepticism is evidence that an adult "doesn't get" 21st century learning. Back in the 1980s, parents were befuddled by high schoolers who could manage the tricky feat of talking on the phone for hours while playing Atari. Yet, happily, few adults mistook these pursuits for learning or thought the kids in question had mastered new, valuable skills. A student using an iPad to consult Wikipedia to find a description of the Harlem Renaissance is, other things equal, learning no more than did a student 25 years ago who used an encyclopedia to find the same information—except that the ability to digitally cut and paste can make it even easier for today's students to avoid processing knowledge into long-term memory.

Joel Rose, founder of New York City's School of One and the national hybrid school designer New Classrooms, explains, "Many of our technological capabilities . . . are either inaccessible or clumsily grafted on. Three computers added to the back of a classroom may look like a positive step toward bringing that classroom into the advanced technological age. However, smoothly integrating three computers into a daily lesson is not always easy when a teacher has to consider the needs of 28 students all learning at the same time."[13] The National Center for Education Statistics for instance, has reported that, while 99% of teachers have access to computers in the classroom, only 40% of them claim to use the computers often; 10% say they never use them.[14]

MOORESVILLE GRADED SCHOOL DISTRICT: FISH DON'T TALK ABOUT WATER

When fish gather for an evening of leisure around the reef, we imagine they don't spend a lot of time talking about how remarkable it is that they live in the water. We suppose they might chat about water quality, scenic vistas, scary predators, and delightful meals, but we doubt they spend much time saying, "Hey, how crazy is it that we live underwater?" We feel confident saying this because we know hardly anybody who spends a lot of time saying, "How crazy is it that we walk around breathing air?"

The relevance of this little aside? When we are talking to school and system leaders who really know what they're doing with technology, we're always struck by how little they talk about technology. Like the fish, they take the medium they swim in for granted; their focus is on the students and the learning.

Starting in 2007, Mooresville, North Carolina, moved to issue laptops to all fourth- to 12th-graders and licensed staff, provided 24-hour access, and adopted smartboards in all K–3 classrooms. At the same time, Mooresville's website goes out of its way to caution, "Technology alone is not a panacea, thus the real focus is how we engage our students with this instructional tool to get results and add value to their academic performance."[15] The *New York Times* has reported that the system's teachers and administrators say they value technology not for the "newest content" but for helping educators wrestle with student "curiosity, boredom, embarrassment, angst" and "deliver what only people can."[16]

Students in a Mooresville classroom

Superintendent Mark Edwards says, "This is not about the technology. It's not about the box. It's about changing the culture of instruction."[17] This has all paid off, big time. In 2013, *Scholastic Administrator* named Mooresville the best school system in the country, and the American Association of School Administrators named Edwards the nation's superintendent of the year.

As Edwards tells it, the district took pains to put learning solutions first, and then used technology to implement them in an affordable way. He says, "We melted the walls. We redesigned the classrooms. We don't have straight rows. We don't buy desks anymore. We only buy tables, and we aligned them so that the teacher is really moving." Classrooms don't have a traditional "front" and "back" because teachers are circulating or teaching from the middle of the classroom. This sounds a lot like what should happen when we apply learning science to classroom design, with an eye to engaging all students in deliberate practice and providing timely feedback. Indeed, it's what dynamic instructors have been doing and recommending for decades, with technology helping to make such instruction more feasible in more classrooms. Remember, technology doesn't change the rules for learning; it just complements it.

But Edwards makes it clear that the technology is complementary to the district's focus on instruction and pedagogy. Edwards says, "We focused on achievement from day one, so we've had formative data meetings throughout the year, and we look at classes, schools, individual students. On a regular basis our teachers are talking about their work. They've had a 1% raise in four years, and yet morale is real high because they were successful."

In classes, teachers are expected to focus on practice and feedback, rather than lecturing. As Edwards relates, "One visitor said, 'You know, I just spent three hours in the school and didn't see one teacher teaching to a class.' I told them, 'You might stay here a week and not see that.' The teacher will give an overview of what we're working on and then there will be a project group over there working on one thing and individual students working." Edwards has said he expects "a teacher . . . will deftly move among tables of students, listening and observing intently, then engaging as needed with groups or individual students. It's a physical approach to teaching, but the benefits of proximity are truly significant."[18]

When it comes to assessment, Mooresville focuses on rapid feedback, making it an integral part of the instructional process. Edwards says, "An observer just yesterday was watching a teacher give a formative assessment, when somebody asked the teacher, 'When will you get this back?' The teacher said, 'Well, if you give me 10 seconds, I'll have it back.' It's this immediacy of information and the level of precision that is stunning.

Students in a Mooresville classroom

At any time, teachers can articulate to any parent or student, with exacting detail, how the student is doing. That's absolutely impossible without the digital resources."

When vendors come calling, Mooresville insists on piloting even the most promising tools before adopting anything. Edwards explains that if a cool-seeming tool comes up short, either on performance or on ease of use, Mooresville passes. He says, "If something doesn't cut it in a couple of years, it's time to make room for something else."

Mooresville's track record since it began its digital conversion in late 2007 suggests that this kind of approach can pay big dividends. Between 2007 and 2012, proficiency on core-subject state exams in reading, math, and science rose from 68% to 89%, the graduation rate increased by 14 points to 91%, and the share of graduates attending a two- or four-year college rose from 75% to 88%.[19] Meanwhile, in 2011–12, Mooresville ranked third in the state for graduation rates and second in student test scores, while ranking only 100 out of 115 districts in per pupil spending, with annual outlays of $7,400 per student.[20]

But "success" goes beyond improvement in student performance. One Mooresville teacher explained, "I think 'expectation' is the right word. . . . The expectation is, 'Here is your laptop, and you will learn how to use it.'"[21] Mooresville High School Principal Todd Wirt has said of Edwards, "He just doesn't allow anybody around him to make excuses or build obstacles."[22] Leaders in Mooresville say would-be imitators need "leaders who see budget and procedural restrictions as obstacles to be conquered, not feared."[23]

Edwards says that the culture of teaching has been transformed: "Two years ago we asked the teachers to come to the summer institute for the grand fee of $50. This is a three-day training session, so it was really nothing more than a token payment. This past year we had 94% attendance. So the teachers have bought into it. Another key thing is that we really worked at and were thoughtful about building the cultural aspects of this. We looked at the culture within the school community, the student community, and the teacher community. Now, if someone's not onboard, they really stick out. The staff feels like, 'Wow, what's wrong with that person?'"

In his popular book *Every Child, Every Day*, Edwards sums up Mooresville's goal for its digital conversion: "We are not trying to add on to old ways of teaching and learning. Rather, we are trying to 'rethink school' from the ground up, enabled by today's technologies and guided by the demands of the 21st-century workplace."[24]

TECHNOLOGY CAN BE A POWERFUL TOOL

Recall our two historical examples of powerful early learning "technologies," the book and the Socratic method. The book helps learning by providing relief to working memory—students don't have to remember everything a lecturer tells them; they have a source to review and return to. Yet the book is a fixed medium—it says the same thing in the same way to every learner who approaches it. The Socratic method helps learning by providing high-quality practice and feedback, personalized to the learner's own stage of understanding. Yet it is an ephemeral experience—you have to remember what happened to you during the questioning.

Today's technology offers the prospect of getting the best of both of these approaches into new learning environments. Adaptive learning environments can be repeatedly accessed to retrace ground that's been covered before, while providing the challenge that all learners need, when they need it. This has the potential to provide the best of both worlds.

This is why it's exciting to think about bringing technology the right way into students' and teachers' lives, tapping into learning science while taking advantage of what technology can do.

Joel Rose, founder of national hybrid school designer New Classrooms mentioned a few pages back, observes that technology can "allow us to re-imagine new combinations of educator expertise, time, instructional materials, research, physical space, parental support, and (yes) technology in ways that achieve optimal outcomes for students. . . . [Through] a combination of teacher-led instruction, student collaborative activities, software, virtual instructors, and a complex scheduling algorithm [we can now] enable each student to move through an individualized learning progression at his or her own pace."[25]

Technology can be a terrific resource—as in Mooresville—if we start with the learning problems, find better solutions to them, and use technology to make those solutions more affordable, reliable, available, customizable, and data-rich. This is the essence of good learning engineering—not to jump at every cool idea that floats across the ed-tech ether, but rather to be aware of how your current learning environments are missing something better for learning, and looking at new technologies to see if any of them can make better solutions feasible at scale.

Approaching technology with a focus on learning solutions helps ensure that schools and systems don't waste money on cool-looking yet ineffectual products—and, perhaps even more important, helps avoid wasting teacher and student time. In Chapter 5, we'll look at how to think about this at a larger scale.

NOTES

1. Fullan, M. (2011, May). *Choosing the wrong drivers for whole system reform*. Centre for Strategic Education Seminar Series. Paper No. 204. p. 15.

2. Horn, M. (2012). No shock as Peru's one-to-one laptops miss mark. *Forbes*. Retrieved from http://www.forbes.com

3. Greenstein, S., & Devereux, M. *The crisis at Encyclopedia Britannica* (Report No. 5-306-504). Evanston, IL: Northwestern University. Retrieved from http://www.kellogg.northwestern.edu/faculty/green stein/images/htm/Research/Cases/EncyclopaediaBritannica.pdf

4. Evans, P., & Wurster, T. S. (2000). *Blown to bits: How the new economics of information transforms strategy*. Boston, MA: Harvard Business School Press.

5. Stross, R. (2009, May 2). Encyclopedic knowledge, then vs. now. *New York Times*. Retrieved from http://www.nytimes.com

6. Evans, P., & Wurster, T. S. (2000). *Blown to bits: How the new economics of information transforms strategy*. Boston, MA: Harvard Business School Press.

7. Cohen, N. (2009, March 30). Microsoft Encarta dies after long battle with Wikipedia. *New York Times.* Retrieved from http://www.nytimes.com

8. Ash, Katie. (2012, May 8). Idaho education chief defends reforms. *Education Week.* http://blogs.edweek.org/edweek/DigitalEducation/2012/05/tom_luna_unpacks_the_idaho_ed_.html

9. IDEO. (2009). A design-thinking approach to public school for Henry Ford Learning Institute. Retrieved from http://www.ideo.com/work/a-design-thinking-approach-to-public-school

10. Brown, T. (2008, June). Design thinking. *Harvard Business Review.* p. 4. Retrieved from http://www.unusualleading.com/wp-content/uploads/2009/12/HBR-on-Design-Thinking.pdf

11 In conversation with Adam Masur, March 26, 2012.

12. Bloom, M. (2012, December 5). Some educators question whether iPads are the solution to everything. *StateImpact.* Retrieved from http://stateimpact.npr.org/ohio/2012/12/05/some-educators-question-whether-ipads-are-the-solution-to-everything/

13. Rose, J. (2012, May 9). How to break free of our 19th-century factory-model education system. *The Atlantic.* Retrieved from http://www.theatlantic.com

14. National Center for Education Statistics. (2009). *Teachers' use of educational technology in U.S. public schools.* http://nces.ed.gov/pubs2010/2010040.pdf

15. Digital conversion executive summary. (2012). Retrieved from http://www5.mgsd.k12.nc.us/staffsites/digitalconversion/Digital_Conversion//MGSD_Digital_Conversion.html

16. Schwarz, A. (2012, February 12). Mooresville's shining example (it's not just about the laptops). *New York Times.* Retrieved from http://www.nytimes.com.

17. Schwarz, A. (2012, February 12). Mooresville's shining example (it's not just about the laptops). *New York Times.* Retrieved from http://www.nytimes.com.

18. Mark Edwards. (2012, February). Our digital conversion. *School Administrator, 69*(2), 20–24. http://www.aasa.org/content.aspx?id=21680

19. Edwards, M. (2012). Mooresville Graded School District's digital conversion. Retrieved from http://www.mgsd.k12.nc.us/MGSD/Our District_files/Presentation%20%28August%29.pdf

20. Quillen, I. (2011, October 17). Building the digital district. *Education Week.* Retrieved from http://www.edweek.org

21. Quillen, I. (2011, October 17). Building the digital district. *Education Week.* Retrieved from http://www.edweek.org

22. Quillen, I. (2011, October 17). Building the digital district. *Education Week.* Retrieved from http://www.edweek.org

23. Quillen, I. (2011, October 17). Building the Digital District. *Education Week.* Retrieved from http://www.edweek.org

24. Edwards, M. (2014). *Every child, every day: A digital conversion model for student achievement.* New York, NY: Pearson. p. 3.

25. Rose, J. (2012, May 9). How to break free of our 19th-century factory-model education system. *The Atlantic.* Retrieved from http://www.theatlantic.com

CHAPTER 5

Redesigning Schools and Systems

Words like "innovative," "21st century skills," and "hybrid learning environments" all sound very cool. Unless we're paying careful attention, that impressive-sounding jargon can stand in for simpler questions we should be asking about how we're using new tools to make sure kids are learning more, better, and more richly.

Smart redesign doesn't require technology. For instance, the KIPP Academies provide an impressive low-tech example of learning-enabled redesign. KIPP is a nationally acclaimed network of more than 100 charter schools with more than 41,000 students across the United States focused on serving at-risk populations. Since being founded by teachers Mike Feinberg and Dave Levin in 1994, KIPP has posted some impressive results.[1]

KIPP puts key elements of learning science to work, even without the aid of new technologies (truth be told, we're not even sure they have always done this intentionally). They put what we know about motivation to work in purposeful and intense ways. For example, KIPP asks students to repeatedly visualize and talk about making it to college. As we saw in Chapter 2, getting students to value the outcomes they're working toward fuels learning. KIPP relentlessly tells its students, "You can do this," and selects teachers in large part for their willingness to strategize with students on how to succeed. That "no excuses" approach to schooling helps deal with both the self-efficacy and attribution motivation problems we discussed in Chapter 2. KIPP's extended day and year mean that students are deeply immersed in this supportive culture and in learning activities that promote KIPP's aims.

It's not just motivation—KIPP taps into other invaluable elements of learning science. The KIPP model entails copious amounts of practice, accommodated by substantial added learning time. Students are taught to keep their eyes on whoever is speaking to them. This not only communicates respect, but it also increases the odds that working memory and conscious attention will be focused on the speaker and whatever the speaker is talking about.

As the KIPP example suggests, redesign should start with identifying learning problems and putting learning science to work in tackling them. Technology then emerges as a set of tools that can help with this work, taking good learning solutions and making them more affordable, reliable, available, customizable, and data-rich.

Peter Cohen, chief executive of Pearson School, a top publisher of classroom texts and software, says of the typical school or system leader when it comes to buying education technology products, "They want the shiny new one. . . . They always want the latest, when other things have been proven the longest and demonstrated to get results."[2] Especially when new entrants come equipped with big ideas and cool words, it can be all too easy to focus on the sizzle rather than the steak. As Jack Schneider, assistant professor at the College of the Holy Cross, has observed, "Funding projects to improve teacher training, development, and retention is less sexy than cutting the ribbon on a lab full of lightning-fast computers."[3]

There are few one-size-fits-all learning technologies. Rather, the right technology solutions will depend on the needs of *your* students and teachers. Anthony Kim, CEO of Education Elements, relates, "One big district was telling us about an Algebra I program that they purchased for their ninth-graders and how it didn't work." After discussing the matter, Kim says, "We found out that the product they selected was 'level-set' for ninth-graders, and their kids were reading at a third- or fourth-grade level. So there was not even a chance for these kids to be successful using this product." Kim says that districts need to start by carefully identifying their needs but often fail to do so. The result, he says, is that, "Often, when schools are making these decisions, they're thinking, 'I need an Algebra I class' and 'I need it online,' without thinking about where their students are or what scaffolding they need to make it work."

DESIGNING FOR NEW CHALLENGES AND OPPORTUNITIES

Learning engineers step back from conventional assumptions about schools and teachers to ask how we might reengineer what schools and teachers do to profoundly improve teaching and learning.

Public school systems, of course, have firmly embedded cultures drenched with strong assumptions about who will teach, what classrooms look like, and how systems will operate. There are rules, regulations, and routines that shape the calendar, "bell schedules" (how anachronistic does *that* sound to a modern student?), curriculum, class size policies, collective bargaining agreements, teacher job descriptions, and much else. New technologies have generally been folded into these established routines rather than used as a chance to rethink them.

As one of your coauthors has previously observed in the *The Same Thing Over and Over:*

> From 1647, when Massachusetts enacted the first educational statute in the American colonies, it took a little over three centuries to build a school system that enrolled three-quarters of our youth on a regular basis. During this time, schools were expected to mold youth into God-fearing, authority-respecting citizens with little concern for academic performance or promoting economic opportunity.
>
> Just when we figured out how to enroll most children in schooling—well into the twentieth century—the pool of talented female labor that had been sustaining those schools for almost a hundred years began to thin out. Simultaneously, values that had undergirded those schools started to dissolve amid changing cultural norms. We radically expanded the number of teachers we hired; repurposed schools to address the legacy of slavery and racial inequality; redefined the moral purpose of schools from promoting "Americanism" to appreciating diversity and tolerance; within a generation, proceeded to declare education the "new civil right"; promised to educate every child to a high level of proficiency; and asked schools to equalize opportunity so that all students might have a chance to succeed in a knowledge-based economy.[4]

Today, we're asking schools to do something that they were never designed to do. We also have new capabilities that were unimaginable when yesterday's reformers were crafting the schools that we still inhabit. Redesigning schooling to meet new challenges with old and new tools requires that we unpack learning goals and approaches and ask whether there are smarter, better ways to promote learning.

Consider that the most important thing schools can offer is terrific teaching and that the talent pool on which schooling draws has changed profoundly in recent decades. This suggests the value of rethinking our assumptions about how schools ought to attract and use talent. After all, since schools no longer enjoy a monopoly on educated women, they need to find new ways to recruit and retain skilled teachers. Sixty years ago, more than half of all college-educated women became teachers; today, it's closer to 15%. And we have to expect folks will change careers more frequently, too: 40 years ago, the average college grad expected to hold perhaps five jobs in the course of his career; today's grads expect to hold that many jobs by the age of 30. New labor market realities and expectations mean we need to rethink our assumptions about how we can and should prepare and use instructional talent.[5]

Unbundling "Teaching" and "Schooling"

Despite these dramatic changes, schooling and teaching today look remarkably the way they did a century ago. One would not say that about medicine, engineering, farming, air travel, or package delivery. In these fields, dramatic shifts in the labor force, management practices, technology, and communications transformed familiar institutions and comfortable routines into more efficient and more effective versions of themselves.

These transformative gains have generally not been a product of doing the same things in the same way, only with more elbow grease. Rather, they have been the result of rethinking the way the work is done to meet our goals. Instead of one doctor serving as general practitioner, surgeon, ophthalmologist, and pharmacist, the profession (in concert with training and technology) evolved to permit these functions to be unbundled and then reassembled in smarter ways. This makes it possible to take fuller advantage of expertise and technological advances, though it poses new challenges of coordination.

Familiar, mundane advances like buying plane tickets online or using an ATM have made it cheaper and easier for people to travel or access their savings. Rather than requiring travel agents or banks to hire full-time employees to handle many routine tasks during set hours, customers can now accomplish the same tasks at a time of their choosing. This has reduced the amount of time that travel agents or bankers must devote to routine tasks, permitting a smaller number of employees to focus on responsibilities that take full advantage of complex skills that can't be carried out by technology.

Unbundling involves finding ways to deconstruct established structures and routines and reassemble them in new, smarter ways. If we think of schools as evolving institutions charged with helping students master a range of decisions and tasks and keeping them safe for a period of time during the day—rather than as inviolate and immutable places charged with the entirety of teaching and learning—we can find opportunities to unbundle and customize. (If readers are interested, they can find a more extended discussion in coauthor Hess's "'Unbundling' Schools and Schooling" chapter in the 2012 volume *The Futures of School Reform.*[6])

Rethinking What Teachers Do

The most critical factor determining the quality of learning is the quality of instruction. This is why learning engineers take every opportunity to ask how to boost the value, amount, and impact of teaching.

Now, the best teachers have always done some bootstrap learning engineering. One of your coauthors has always had truly execrable penmanship—six-sigma, but the bad way. When he made it to second grade (which required a near-papal dispensation from the principal), he faced with dread a weekly writing assignment given to the whole class. The teacher could see there was no way she could read what he wrote. A recipe for disaster? Not so. This teacher started with her goal, which was structured communication, not "handwriting." Then she made him a deal: He could give the entire class a short, graded, verbal presentation (with visuals!) every week instead. She focused on what the real objective was, what the constraint was, and then customized the practice and feedback accordingly. No technology was involved (except a rather cool device that projected images from books onto a screen), just the work of a master learning engineer. Your coauthor mastered the content and developed a sense of efficacy around communication, and the handwriting issue eventually became moot. (Thank heaven for keyboards!)

The trick is to apply creative problem solving on a broader level. For starters, rather than assuming that teachers in a school or system continue to work similar hours and cover similar content in similar-looking classrooms, learning engineers ask how we might rethink things to make the best use of teachers' varied talents and strengths. This may mean thinking more about specialization; team teaching; new roles; the interplay of people and technology; and more fundamental differentiation of learning experience, scope, sequence, and pacing.

Other professions operate in ways that make it easier to squeeze maximum value out of their most talented and most highly trained professionals. The medical field is an example: The American Medical Association now recognizes 199 specialties. While there are 7 million medical professionals in the United States, fewer than 1 million are physicians.[7] The rest are trained practitioners with talents that complement those of doctors. In a well-run medical practice, surgeons don't spend much time filling out minutiae in patient charts or negotiating with insurance companies; these responsibilities are left to others who are adept at this.

If schools embrace specialization among teachers and staff, they can strategically rearrange them. New York City's School of One is an intriguing example of how this kind of thinking can play out. The School of One is a model of math instruction for Grades 6 through 8 that abandons the traditional classroom in favor of orchestrating multiple modalities of instruction for each student, such as live, teacher-led lessons, software-based lessons, collaborative activities, virtual tutors, and individual practice. The school identifies which learning objective a student ought to master next and then assigns the student to a complementary learning experience for each unit based on each student's needs, history, and learning capability. This lets teachers customize what a student learns each day on the basis of what he has already mastered and needs to learn, doing so with an eye toward the ways that he learns best, and the efficient use of school resources. Each day's instruction is different, yet better for each student.

Rather than employ a conventional curricular scope and sequence for an entire class, the School of One unpacks each grade level's math objectives into its component parts. Think of an iPod rather than an old LP record. Fifty years ago, if you wanted to listen to your favorite song, you would buy the LP, lay it on your turntable, and likely as not sit through the whole album from the beginning until your song played. Like you, everyone else who wanted to hear a particular song on that record had to buy the same LP in order to hear it. However, with the advent of digital music technology, listeners no longer have to purchase the whole album to get their favorite songs; they can buy each song individually and then create a customized playlist. Just as technology helped audiophiles custom-fit their music to suit their listening preferences, it can help educators custom-fit lesson plans and instruction material to their students. The School of One organizes instruction using this intuition. It uses pretests; brief, near-daily unit assessments; a slew of instructional modalities (large group, small group, online tutoring, computer-assisted, and so on); and an organizing algorithm to customize scope and sequence to each student's individual learning needs.

In the School of One, students skip over objectives they've already mastered and learn different objectives using the instructional approaches deemed most appropriate for them. They spend more time on certain learning objectives when they need to and race ahead when they are able. In many ways, the School of One is simply using technology to facilitate and make practical an amped-up version of the student-centered instruction that Ted Sizer and Deborah Meier were touting decades ago in books like *Horace's Compromise* and *The Power of Their Ideas.*[8] By combining all math instruction into a common, flexible enterprise, it becomes possible for teachers to differentiate instruction, share instructional responsibilities, and collaborate in ways that are usually impractical.

The School of One suggests a number of intriguing possibilities. Just for starters, teachers nationally are typically absent seven or eight days a year. In most classrooms, learning is put on pause during those days. The School of One design means an absent teacher no longer stops students from learning. This change, all by itself, effectively adds about seven or eight days of real instructional time per year. The School of One also enables individual teachers to do more of what they do best. One member of a school math team might handle all of the instruction in a particular sub-domain, building her expertise while allowing colleagues to similarly focus on what they do best. The integration of multiple modalities lets some instruction be delivered via online tutoring or intensive computer-assisted exercises, freeing teachers to devote more time to small-group instruction, personal coaching, and other roles that they are uniquely equipped to tackle.

Indeed, freeing up teacher time makes it increasingly possible to think about redesigning the profession itself. Instead of every teacher having to spend six hours a day in a classroom explaining things to students, it becomes easier to envision varied roles for teaching professionals. In medicine, the all-encompassing "doctor" of 1900 has given way to 200 specialties today, complemented by millions of trained personnel who work as registered nurses or emergency medical technicians. It's similarly possible to envision the staid job of "teacher" evolving into a raft of opportunities that allow educators to grow, take on new challenges, do more of what they do best, and garner the prestige and compensation that follow.

Putting the Principles of Redesign to Work

As important as it is to rethink the role of teachers, school redesign is inevitably a broader challenge. When it comes to doing redesign right, a learning engineer sees a wealth of opportunities to do better. For illustrative purposes, let's touch on a few.

School improvement. One place where high expectations often go unfulfilled is with school improvement or "turnaround" efforts. Strategies for "turning around" low-performing schools are nothing new. They were the goal of Comprehensive School Reform in the early 1990s and of the reconstitution provisions of No Child Left Behind in 2001. More recently, they have been the focus of the federal School Improvement Grant (SIG) program. Yet all of this activity and spending have a disappointing and rather uneven record of improving schools and student outcomes. Common challenges include a limited pool of talented faculty, at-risk student populations with high rates of discipline problems and apathy, a culture of low expectations, and a question as to how school leaders can jump-start the transformation to a new way of doing business.

A learning engineer wouldn't start a school improvement effort by deciding on the technologies to be used—that would be like a general physician deciding to give a patient an artificial hip, even if the patient's got strep throat. A persistent headache for turnaround leaders is that it is hard to take the steps that often seem essential to actually turning around a school. For instance, many turnarounds are focused on attracting more terrific teachers

and providing more student learning time. But the practical challenges of finding those teachers and providing that time can be
steep. That's where technology can help. If it's difficult to find
enough skilled teachers locally, virtual instruction might help
remedy the problem and provide the opportunity for students to
take courses that the school might not otherwise provide. If students need more remediation and support, one-one-one virtual
tutors or computerized tutoring systems (of the kind discussed in
Chapter 3) can help.

There's also a need to plan for what happens after any short-
term infusion of turnaround funds goes away: Are any changes
creating new ongoing costs, or will the new model prove sustainable over time? Substituting reusable tutoring systems or taking
advantage of virtual offerings can make it possible to sustain
offerings that would otherwise disappear when lost SIG dollars
mean a school can't retain extra staff.

Professional learning communities (PLCs). As far as we can
tell, nearly every school in America either claims to be a PLC or
says it wants to be one. They all seek to provide collaborative planning time, use data to make instructional decisions, and forge cultures of professional practice. Yet the reality is that most PLCs fail
to deliver the hoped-for results or even to look a whole lot like
what proponents might desire. What's going wrong? Well, it's
tough to find sufficient planning time. Data often arrive too slowly
and in too bulky a form to thoroughly drive instruction. Too few
teachers have the knowledge or skill to really wield data as effectively as they might.

A professional learning community is a way to get teachers to
regularly and repeatedly work together. That's a terrific notion—
but it's only a start. A learning engineer starts by getting more
precise about the challenges at hand and then determines
whether there's a role for technology in addressing them. For
instance, a familiar problem is that grade-level teams assign common assessment to their charges only every four to six weeks. That
makes it difficult to talk in depth about daily and weekly mastery.
However, a new online platform, MasteryConnect, has made it
possible for teachers to quickly and easily locate a wealth of K–12
reading and math assessments and to instantly grade them using
a laptop's built-in camera. This allows a team to readily assign and

discuss a common formative assessment on a weekly, or even a daily, basis. At the same time, plain old social media can allow that grade-level team to meet and plan virtually—so they can find more time to check in on a Sunday night, or on a weeknight when time is limited and teachers need to hustle home to get their kids to soccer practice.

Differentiating instruction. A building block for instructional improvement is the push to "differentiate instruction." This involves teachers identifying individual student needs and teaching to those in appropriate ways. The trick, of course, is that doing so can be an enormously challenging task for a fourth-grade teacher with 28 kids and even more so for a high school teacher who sees 150 students a day. The result is that differentiation is often more an aspiration than a reality.

Differentiating learning to match student motivation and previous mastery makes obvious sense. However, expecting individual teachers to differentiate among 28 or more kids is asking a lot. This is precisely where technology can make a big difference. A learning engineer can use granular, real-time data to modify and alter the instructional environments to make it easier for students to get instruction, practice, and feedback at their own pace and matched to their particular needs. Part of the beauty of a Carpe Diem or a School of One is that the design of the school facilitates differentiation; students are no longer bundled into classrooms moving at approximately the same pace through a generic curricular scope or sequence (with teachers doing their best to differentiate along the way). Now, the differentiation is baked into the very fabric of the classroom and the school. This makes things easier on the teacher.

Of course, you may be most concerned at the moment not with any of the above but with STEM instruction, Common Core implementation, multiple pathways, summer reading loss, or much else. The point is that all of these problems become more tractable if you approach them like a learning engineer, using what's known about learning and the surrounding constraints to craft smarter solutions. As you do so, it's always useful to explore whether technology can help you design solutions that are more (go ahead, say it with us) . . . affordable, reliable, available, customizable, and data-rich.

KHAN ACADEMY: DISTINGUISHING
THE APP STORE FROM THE APPS

Many innovations are less earth-shattering than advertised. Remember, for all the excitement about the "flipped classroom," we've actually been flipping classrooms for about five centuries—since the introduction of the book. The Internet has made it possible to do that in new ways, but the underlying idea is not groundbreaking.

The Khan Academy started to bring some real scale and order to making online instructional videos readily and freely available. Let's take a brief look at the Khan Academy, to see if we can use a learning engineer's approach to distinguish the steak from the sizzle—and identify big opportunities to do even better.

The Khan Academy is a free online resource that provides a wealth of video lectures on a number of science and math topics. It was born when Salman Khan, a former hedge fund analyst, created a YouTube account in 2006 to tutor his own nephews and nieces. By the end of 2012, the organization had delivered more than 200 million lesson sessions.[9]

Most Khan lectures feature a "screencast" demonstrating a concept or solution, e.g., to a math problem, with Khan's voice-over explaining what he's doing. For many topics, there are also practice exercises available; those are separately accessed, however, from the videos. The videos and practice can be used by anyone, typically at home. This can reduce the need for teachers to convey information through lectures, freeing up class time for teachers to work with students on problems. The aim is to take the "flipped classroom" logic of the book one step further, with students absorbing content at home and then getting deliberate practice, feedback, motivation, and engagement in the classroom.

In 2012, Khan was named as one of *Time* magazine's 100 most influential people. Bill Gates called him "teacher to the world."[10] Khan Academy isn't just popular, it has many people convinced that it marks a turning point in education, and has generated headlines like "Khan Academy: The future of education?" and "How Khan Academy is changing the rules of education."[11] Tom Vander Ark argues in his book *Getting Smart,* "The reason Khan Academy evolved and now has the reach that it does is because of one simple and powerful thing: The way he teaches works."[12]

Indeed, popular accounts of the Khan Academy tend to wax rhapsodic about the fact that students can now access a library of instructional videos 24/7, without much wondering about the instructional quality or impact of raw videos.

On this point, Khan himself is very clear—he never claimed expertise in learning science, or research on misconceptions in math and science. He was just trying to help his extended family with their kids' math problems, and used technology to make the task easier. Now, it turns out that the simplicity of the thousands of videos he produced, with Khan's voice recorded atop a video of notes sketched on the screen, is consistent with learning science. As we saw in Chapter 2, informal audio on top of a visual that is different from the audio but is matched to the content really can help learning. However, the reason Khan did not, for example, put a distracting video of himself on the screen is not due to a familiarity with learning science—he simply couldn't find a video camera when he started. That's why he just recorded the audio with a screen capture of him writing notes.

Learners watching his videos benefit from this approach, accidental or not. Khan Academy itself is now working with cognitive science researchers, improving the quality of its assessment data, and plans to do more systematic piloting of different approaches to their topics.

While Khan Academy makes it possible to put learning design to better use, there's no more reason to expect that Sal Khan himself would be naturally equipped to create a wealth of great instructional offerings across a wide breadth of topics than it would be to think that the folks who built Apple's App Store were the best candidates to design any particular app. Part of the reason the App Store is a terrific platform is that it allows for a variety of talented people to share their expertise and craftsmanship.

This makes for a dynamic process, fueled by evaluation as well as inventiveness. For instance, in 2012, a pair of associate professors from Michigan's Grand Valley State University took an acerbic look at certain Khan Academy lessons in the course of a video critique (styled after the snide commentary of the cult television favorite *Mystery Science Theater 3000*). As *Education Week*'s Katie Ash reported, "[They] pointed out areas where [Khan] could improve his pedagogy, generally poking fun at the Khan Academy and its trove of videos."[13]

The Khan Academy responded by modifying its offerings. The back-and-forth illustrated the ability of technology to make such interaction more transparent and rapid, enabling Khan's offering to benefit from dispersed expertise. Such healthy back-and-forth, made possible in an online environment, offers the promise that new tools can be more systematically refined over time. In short, we shouldn't be pro-Khan or anti-Khan. Rather, we should appreciate both the innovations of the Khan Academy and tough-minded scrutiny of its content. The Khan "app store" ultimately provides opportunities to craft smarter, ever-better instructional unit "apps" that will ideally also include well-designed deliberate practice and timely feedback.

LEVERAGING THE ELEMENTS OF LEARNING DESIGN

A focus on learning science makes it easier to think through how new tools or technologies can be purposefully employed.

Structure matters. Good instruction requires well-designed objectives, assessments, practice and feedback, demonstrations, information, and overviews. A given learning tool (like Khan Academy instruction) can help with some of these, but it needs to be clear how it fits into a fully articulated instructional unit. If these components aren't clearly supported by evidence, or if it's not clear how the pieces fit together, be wary. For example, Khan videos can help mightily with the information and demonstration elements, but they don't currently provide requisite practice and feedback. A well-structured learning solution addresses that. Whether you're eyeballing an app for a handheld, a new classroom tool, or a new version of a textbook that brags "now with a website!" be sure to ask where each piece fits, and what else may be needed to complete the instructional experience.

This is true with or without technology, of course. For example, Big Picture Learning is a network of about 50 nontraditional schools across the country. The best-known of these is "The Met" in Providence, Rhode Island. At Big Picture, each student's learning experience features an extensive (low-tech) internship experience through which the student is connected to a mentor. San Diego-based High Tech High has something similar: In ninth and tenth grades, students shadow adults through their workdays. Juniors complete semester-long internships, and seniors develop projects on problems of community concern. These experiences offer terrific opportunities for applied practice and feedback, but they need to be connected to a fully articulated instructional experience (with objectives, practice, assessments, and the rest) if we're going to have confidence that students are going to build long-term mastery.

Especially for those schools or systems unsure about how to institute virtual learning, one option is to partner with an existing virtual school that already knows what it's doing. The biggest and most famous virtual school operating in the United States today, for instance, is the Florida Virtual School (FLVS). Founded in 1997, FLVS now serves students K–12 and provides virtual classes to students all over the country. In 2013–14, FLVS employed more than 2,000 educators and served more than 400,000 students in dozens of subjects.[14]

Personalization matters. Depending on a student's previous mastery, what comes simply to one student may be a confusing struggle for another. This is the challenge that "differentiated instruction" seeks to address. Tools that help identify what students have already mastered in long-term memory make it easier to customize demonstrations, practice, and feedback. Sure, one-to-one human tutors can help with this—but, as we've noted several times, this approach can run into problems of cost and scale. This is where those intelligent tutoring systems can help so much.

Technology makes customization possible, even as it can make the teacher's role more manageable. Scott Kinney, senior vice president at Discovery Education, says, "You look at something like differentiated instruction, something that's been around and discussed for many years. It's not that teachers without technology can't differentiate; they can. There are two or three in the school building who would do it and would do a great job. . . . [But] with the tools we have today, it becomes practical for everyone to deliver those kinds of best practices. . . . Instead of a teacher spending the night in the library searching for resources to meet the needs of each individual student, it becomes practical for every educator to employ what we know is a great instructional practice."

DreamBox Learning, an adaptive learning platform for K–5 math instruction, provides millions of individualized learning paths, each one tailored to a student's unique needs. It does this by gauging students on embedded assessments while incorporating everything from response time to keystrokes. It then adapts the level of difficulty, the sequencing of content, the number and type of hints given, and pacing for demonstrations and practice. The program was designed by teachers working alongside engineers to build an adaptive engine. DreamBox CEO Jessie Woolley-Wilson says, "It offers practice with guided instruction, collecting 50,000 data points per student per hour—noting whether a student is hesitating or how they solve the problem. All of that helps fuel the analytic engine. This continuous data collection tailors the learning experience to each student, allowing teachers to maximize every instructional minute." A veteran teacher might use DreamBox to provide some routine practice-and-feedback while she works closely with a handful of students with particular needs. At the same time, a novice might lean on the product to support her lesson in teaching fractions or probabilities—ensuring that the students get solid instruction even if she's still figuring out how to effectively teach that unit. Woolley-Wilson says, "Students who don't have parental support or the best teacher can still have an exceptional learning experience."

Motivation matters. Whether students are motivated to learn makes a huge difference. Crucial is whether students value what they're doing and believe they can do it. Lenny Schad, chief technology officer of Houston Independent School District, is the former chief information officer of Katy Independent School District in Texas, a 62,000-student district recognized for its technological efforts. With regard to those efforts, he says: "The heart of what we did in Katy was increase student engagement, because that's where we lose our kids. For them, devices are not an add-on to their life; it's how they live. Engagement leads to improved student achievement and the other outcomes we want. We have to stop thinking about technology as a commodity solution and instead as part of the classroom experience, like textbooks, paper, and pencil."

ClassDojo, for instance, has devised a tool for helping teachers track and highlight positive student behaviors. With millions of teacher and student users, it enables teachers to easily monitor and track student behaviors in real time. Teachers can award points for demonstrating positive actions, like participating in class discussion and helping others, and subtract them for negative behaviors, like calling out in class or being off-task. It lets teachers display points students accumulate for positive behavior in real time, and can customize parental reports to incorporate important traits like persistence, participation, and curiosity. Founder Sam Chaudhary says, "The teacher is no longer tethered to the front of the class. You can award feedback points even if you're in the cafeteria or around the rest of the school."[15]

Evidence matters. Providing rapid, easy access to good data is critical for personalization and feedback. A variety of new tools provide educators with better ways to capture and access data. The trick is figuring out how to use the data to improve learning outcomes. Providers building such tools with an eye to this challenge include PowerSchool, Spiral Universe, Genius SIS, Infinite Campus, Schoolzilla, and LearnBoost. As Scott Kinney of Discovery Education says, "Formative assessment isn't new; it has been around for decades. . . . But technology gives us the ability to instantly look at results, derive meaning from that data, and more importantly change our instructional practice based on what our students know, can do, and understand."

Schoolzilla is a cloud-based data management platform that makes student data more ubiquitous and actionable. Schoolzilla's first tool, the CST Explorer, is a free platform for visualizing California State Test (CST) data. New York-based Wireless Generation has designed a reading diagnostic for smartphones that can help provide teachers with consistent prompts on how to diagnose and help students who encounter certain common problems on literacy assessments. These tools allow educators to assess student mastery of objectives more rapidly, precisely, and frequently than was once possible, making it feasible to target instruction accordingly.

Teaching matters. We often forget that teachers are imperfect learners too. We seemingly expect them to have superhuman retention after a one-shot in-service or a summertime training program, acting as if that's all they need to deftly pick up new instructional techniques and tools. That's crazy. Everything we've already covered about students applies to teachers as well.

The challenge is especially tough when leaders lack meaningful tools for seeing what teachers actually teach inside their isolated classrooms. Standardized testing gives a sense of the outcomes of an isolated teacher's work but says little about the instructional practices that yielded those results. Similarly, structured observation is another tool that is time consuming to organize and which is plagued by the logistics of coordinating sit-down schedules and a reliance on imperfect recall about what happened during class (as discussed in Chapter 4).

New technologies offer better ways to tackle all this. The 360-degree "fish-eye" cameras pioneered in the Bill & Melinda Gates Foundation's $400 million "Measures of Effective Teaching" study allow teachers to be observed and get feedback even when an observer isn't able to sit through their class. The iObservation system collects, manages, and reports longitudinal data from classroom walk-throughs, teacher evaluations, and teacher observation. Such systems make it easier to determine what successful teachers are doing. As we mentioned in Chapter 4, they can also make it newly possible to provide "game tapes" and coaching for teachers so that, just as if they were athletes, they can refine their performances by watching themselves.

TIPS FOR FINDING LEARNING SOLUTIONS

As Carpe Diem founder and CEO Rick Ogston says: "There's a lot to consider; it's not just about going out and buying stuff. . . . When I first started this I thought if you ask the right questions the vendors will tell you the truth. And sometimes the vendors themselves don't even know the full truth. When you ask whether they can do something, they'll tell you, 'Yeah, we do that.' Then they do a part of what they say they can do. Or they do that, but not exactly. And then you realize what they offer doesn't do anything close to what you wanted."

Economists Aaron Chatterji of Duke University and Ben Jones of Northwestern University have suggested a system for evaluating technology products through rigorous, low-cost evaluations and then sharing that information with the public via something akin to a *Consumer Reports* for education technology.[16] Jones says: "With education technology we have really no particular way to know what works and to evaluate claims."[17] It can be difficult for leaders to know which tools, products, or services work—and which don't.

This is in the future—still, there are places to go hunting now. Go back and check out the "Resources on Learning Science" sidebar in Chapter 2; another good resource is the Johns Hopkins "Best Evidence Encyclopedia" project, started by learning researcher Robert Slavin.[18] The League of Innovative Schools, with more than 2 million students, may prove to be a valuable resource.[19] These are the kinds of resources learning engineers can turn to.

Most state, school, and district staff, reasonably enough, expect the vendors promoting new learning solutions to provide smart guidance on how to use them. All their stuff is built by experts—it says so in the brochure—so they must know what they're doing, right? Unfortunately, in our experience, most companies don't spend a lot of time thinking about what works and what doesn't work according to learning science. It's not because these providers lack for smart people, but because the current marketplace has tended to reward "innovativeness" rather than demonstrated impact on learning.

This creates a chicken-and-egg situation: School and district leaders don't know enough to hold vendors' feet to the fire, and vendors, in turn, respond to the things that school and system leaders do focus on (like technological access, teacher handholding, and decades-long relationships among people in the system). Altering this equation requires leaders to be more demanding with vendors, and to ask different questions of both providers and their own teams.

To get this kind of change going, learning engineers should ask at least five quick questions of vendors and themselves when shopping for new learning solutions:

- *Should we do it?* Is there a learning problem this will alleviate? Or will it leave learning the same but deliver it less expensively or more quickly? This is where a bit of background on the learning sciences can help: Is the technology enabling something that will truly matter for your students?
- *Can we do it?* What about your infrastructure for technology, the skills of your students and staff, the support within your environment? Do people already have the skills they need? If not, how easy will it be to bring those skills up to snuff? Is the vendor ready to help support a pilot to help shake out any wrinkles you can't see up front?

- *How do we do it?* What does the training look like? Has it been done successfully in places that resemble your school or system? If not, are you ready to be the guinea pig? If so, will the provider acknowledge that in some way, with free or inexpensive support and whatever else is needed?
- *What if we can't do it?* What are the vendor's support options and methods? How have they handled difficulties, either technical or otherwise, in the past? Is there a vibrant user community that already includes schools like yours?
- *Can we afford it?* This is the money question. It's not just about the cost of purchasing but also related costs for setup, support, training, and staff time. Is it going to be worth it? What are the true costs, and how do they compare to the projected benefits? Is this the best use of limited funds?

Dennis Villano, director of technology integration at Burlington Public Schools in Massachusetts, which employs a one-to-one iPad program, says, "You really have to be careful about looking at what [vendors] are trying to sell. There's no question that ed-tech has exploded over the last couple years in terms of how many products are offered—and there's a lot of money in it right now. But we're pretty focused on the goal, which is creating better, more engaging classrooms. And so we don't have to buy everything that's out there."

ROCKETSHIP EDUCATION: THE ENGINEER'S TALE

When *60 Minutes* or the *New York Times* starts waxing rhapsodic about some exciting new school model and funders start dangling dollars, it's easy to get distracted from what matters. It's especially easy to forget that, when successful, these ventures typically succeed because of the rethinking—not because of the technology. This applies to the Khan Academy, to Mooresville, and to Carpe Diem; another illuminating example is Rocketship Education.

Founded in 2006 by entrepreneur, teacher, and engineer John Danner, Rocketship Education is a network of elementary charter schools that integrate computer-assisted learning in order to personalize instruction and offer additional learning time as part of an affordable model. The schools have used technology to devise smarter ways to assess student needs, customize instruction, and provide additional intensive practice time.

A student and teacher at Rocketship

Rocketship employs a blended model of classroom instruction, drawing heavily on real-time assessments as well as computer-assisted and paraprofessional support in a "learning lab." During the school day, students typically spend five or six hours in a conventional classroom, and another two hours working on a computer in the learning lab, using a program that adapts exercises and tutoring based on student proficiency. Tutors offer additional help to those who need it. Progress is constantly assessed to help teachers identify areas where students need extra support. This is all done with an emphasis on allowing each student to move at his or her own pace.

In 2012, Rocketship Education was the highest-performing public school system for low-income students in the state of California.[20] Because computer-assisted instruction reduces the number of expensive full-time staff that a school requires, Rocketship can deliver its additional instruction and support without additional per-pupil funds. Rocketship expanded to Milwaukee in 2013; as of 2013, Washington, DC, Indianapolis, New Orleans, and Tennessee had each approved eight or more Rocketship schools. Meanwhile, Rocketship has been approved to open 20 new schools in its birthplace, San Jose.[21]

When discussing Rocketship, pundits and observers tend to get caught up in the technology. Danner, sounding like the teacher (he holds an MEd from Vanderbilt) and the engineer he is (he holds a BA and an MA in electrical engineering from Stanford University), says most observers are focusing on the wrong things. "They confuse technology with learning," he says. "We've found that the delivery side of it is considerably less important than figuring out what a kid knows and what they should learn next." In designing Rocketship, he says, the focus was on using technology to assess mastery and provide additional practice time—not to deliver conventional lessons with technology.

Danner explains the personal roots of this approach, saying, "When I was teaching, the thing I got right was that I figured out how to assess kids and how to do an individualized learning plan for every kid. I asked, 'What do they know and what do they need to learn the next day?' That was the core idea of Rocketship. All the technology is, well, 'afterthought' is probably the wrong word, but the technology is relatively unimportant. What a kid knows now and what they need to learn next is probably 80% of our impact, while using this curriculum or tutor is probably 20%."

Danner continues, "Do people understand that about our model? No, not at all. The media wants to tell a story that teaching is going to be replaced by technology, because that's sensational. And that's what people hear about. So, when superintendents and others look at us, they ask the wrong question. They ask us, 'Which online curriculum we are using?' So we tell them, of course, and then they go buy it. But, you know, the actual answer is, if you just apply curricular black boxes to kids, you're not going to get much effect. None of them are good enough at diagnosing where kids are at academically or what they need. But when we tell the media this, they literally ignore all of it."

Inside a Rocketship classroom

Discussing the evolution of Rocketship, Danner explains that the design process started with a focus on outcomes and assessment, and only then moved on to information and practice: "The first thing we did was get really good at assessment. Over the years, we've spent a lot of time with paper and pencil, online, whatever, just trying to find ways to figure out what kids know. So we put a huge amount of effort into just raw assessment. Then, from year one, we worked on building an 'if-then' tool: if a kid has this knowledge map, here's the next most important thing for them to learn. Those are the things that have a significant impact, especially on the lowest quartile and the highest quartile kids, where individualization is the most important. Now we've also invested tons of money in tutoring and things like that, but that's kind of the window dressing as opposed to the meat."

Technology allows Rocketship to customize instruction, provide intensive assessment, and deliver additional targeted practice, at scale. As Danner says, "When we started doing individualization, we were doing what I did in my classroom which was rely on paper and pencil assessment. We did as well as we could. But, practically, that kind of thing is difficult to implement at any scale. Within the first year, we started to do tutoring for the bottom quartile of kids. Then we began to automate the developmental lessons, to put them online. If you think about our progression, it was going from paper and pencil with loose oversight of kids, to thinking about how you could have the maximum learning impact on a kid. Rocketship's tutoring focus was really us figuring out how to group a set of kids who all have the same needs at the same time, in order to get a bigger instructional impact. Computer assessment and computer-assisted instruction was just a question of, 'Can we put kids in a system where, if they make mistakes, they can get computer assistance before having to put their hands up?'"

For Rocketship Education, the design for better learning came first—this "technology" all-star started with paper and pencil, in fact. The technology helped a lot when it came to making the design (sing it with us now) more affordable, reliable, available, customizable, and data-rich—and is now critical to scaling and constantly improving the model. But the real genius of Rocketship is the learning design: The technology is important because it helps enhance that design. Indeed, the tools and algorithms that support models like Rocketship, the School of One, or DreamBox can make it possible to assess, organize, instruct, and support students in a fashion that makes a variety of student-centered school designs newly practical.

Rocketship is constantly looking to grow and evolve its model. One such shift features a plan to modify its separated learning lab structure. Charlie Bufalino, national development associate at Rocketship, told online education technology news outlet *EdSurge*: "The Learning Lab is not going away, rather we are working to integrate its key components directly into our classrooms under the guidance of our incredible teachers and staff."[22] Danner believes that a crucial next step is finding new ways to leverage technology to deliver instruction, just because it is so difficult to get every single teacher to change how he or she teaches within a system that employs thousands of teachers. Constantly identifying challenges and seeking out new ways to do better, Rocketship is a terrific place to look for those seeking to understand the spirit of the learning engineer.

IT'S THE ENGINEERING, NOT THE GIZMOS

It's easy to get caught up in the promise and excitement of new technologies. Who hasn't walked into an Apple store, eyeballed a cutting-edge TV, or stumbled on a new wrist-borne health gizmo and thought, "I want that!" It's natural. And it's easy for us to *imagine* how this new gadget will be a difference maker. Heck, this impulse is what keeps "As Seen on TV" merchants in business.

Lucky for us, learning engineers seek to resist these all-too-human temptations. There are three ways they keep a level head, even as the rest of us drool over the latest Best Buy display.

First, they're meticulous planners. You know how some people say, "I'm a big-picture kind of guy"? Good engineers don't say that. Big-picture guys build a skyscraper but forget to install a fire escape. Engineers don't forget, and they make sure that the escape is accessible from every floor via a clearly marked exit. Big-picture people think, "Wow, that iPad has to be great for learning. I'll buy a lot of them and let our staff figure out what to do with them later—I'm sure it'll turn out great." A learning engineer thinks clearly about the specific learning challenges at hand, and precisely how technology-enhanced solutions can help with them.

Second, learning engineers concentrate on the end goal. They know that no matter the tools, learning is still about helping students use repeated, deliberate practice to exercise working memory and cement components of mastery into long-term memory. It's still about learning environments that do a terrific job of providing information, demonstrations, practice, feedback, assessment, motivation, and the rest, leading to mastery that matters for the long haul.

Third, learning engineers focus on utility when choosing their tools. Powerful learning technologies are those that help educators do these things better, cheaper, faster, or in more precisely targeted ways. Tech-enabled school design is not about vague promises regarding the power of digital learning, but about having a clear idea about how to use new and old technologies, to support better teaching and learning.

Learning engineers lean on learning science and discipline to resist the "As Seen On TV" seductions. Now, in the real world, all this can be tricky to do. There are a number of practical and political complications. In Chapter 6, we'll consider some of those, and how learning engineers can deal with them.

NOTES

1. KIPP Foundation. (2012). The history of KIPP. Retrieved from http://www.kipp.org
2. Gabriel, T., & Richtel, M. (2011, October 8). Inflating the software report card. *New York Times*. Retrieved from http://www.nytimes.com
3. Schneider, Jack. (2011, October 4). Questioning our mania for education technology. *Education Week*. Retrieved from http://www.edweek.org
4. Hess, F. M. (2010). *The same thing over and over: How school reformers get stuck in yesterday's ideas.* Cambridge, MA: Harvard University Press. pp. 191–192.
5. For further discussion of these shifting trends, see Hess, F. M. (2010). *The same thing over and over: How school reformers get stuck in yesterday's ideas.* Cambridge, MA: Harvard University Press. pp. 15–26.
6. Hess, F. M., & Meeks, O. (2012). "Unbundling" schools and schooling. In J. Mehta, R. B. Schwartz, & F. M. Hess, (Eds.), *The futures of school reform.* Cambridge, MA: Harvard Education Press. pp. 95–118.
7. Bureau of Labor Statistics, Occupational employment and wages, 2008, Table 1, http://www.bls.gov/news.release/pdf/ocwage.pdf
8. Sizer, T. R. (1984). *Horace's compromise: The dilemma of the American high school.* New York, NY: Mariner Books; Meier, D. (1995). *The power of their ideas: Lessons for America from a small school in Harlem.* Boston, MA: Beacon Press.
9. Retrieved from http://www.khanacademy.org/
10. CBS News (2012, September 2). Khan Academy: The future of education? Retrieved from http://www.cbsnews.com

11. CBS News (2012, September 2). Khan Academy: The future of education? Retrieved from http://www.cbsnews.com; Thompson, C. (2011, July 15). How Khan Academy Is changing the rules of education. *Wired.* Retrieved from http://www.wired.com

12. Vander Ark, Tom. (2012). *Getting smart: How digital learning is changing the world.* San Francisco, CA: Wiley. p. 68.

13. Ash, K. (2012, July 10.) Critique of Khan Academy goes viral. *Education Week.* Message posted on http://www.blogs.edweek.org

14. *Raising the bar: How education innovation can improve student achievement* [Hearing before the Subcommittee on Early Childhood, Elementary, and Secondary Education, House of Representatives, 2013, testimony of Holly Sagues]. Retrieved from http://edworkforce.house .gov/uploadedfiles/sagues_testimony.pdf

15. Hess, R. (2012). Checking out Class Dojo [Web log post]. Retrieved from http://blogs.edweek.org/edweek/rick_hess_straight_up/2012/ 09/classdojo_a_tool_to_help_teachers_improve_student_behavior .html

16. Chatterji, A., & Jones, B. F. (2012, September). *Harnessing technology to improve K–12 education.* Washington, DC: Brookings Institution. Retrieved from http://www.hamiltonproject.org/files/downloads _and_links/THP_ChatterjiJones_EdTech_DiscPaper.pdf

17. The Hamilton Project. (2012, September 27). *Back to school: Promoting attainment and achievement in K -12 education.* Washington, DC: Brookings Institution.

18. For more information on the Best Evidence Encyclopedia visit http:// education.jhu.edu/research/crre/bee.html

19. For more information on the League of Innovative Schools, see http://www.digitalpromise.org/initiatives/league-of-innovative -schools/

20. Rocketship Education. Academic Performance. Retrieved from http://www.rsed.org/about/Academic-Performance.cfm

21. Layton, L. (2012, July 29). Is a charter school chain called Rocketship ready to soar across America? *Washington Post.* Retrieved from http://www.washingtonpost.com

22. EdSurge. (2013). Are Rocketship's Learning Labs "not really working?" EdSurge News Blurb. January 8, 2013. Posted on https://www .edsurge.com/n/2013-01-08-are-rocketship-s-learning-labs-not -really-working

CHAPTER 6

Doing This in
the Real World

When it comes to improving schools, we hear a lot about what educational leaders *can't* do. One of the coauthors has previously quoted Corinne Gregory, author of *Education Reform and Other Myths*, saying, "Working with schools, it seems to me that there is a great deal of 'can't'-ism going on. And what I have found this to mean is that it is much easier [for leaders] to place blame on 'outside factors' and claim they are helpless to change anything as a result, than it is to actually take the initiative to make their own changes. 'We don't have time.' 'We can't afford it.' 'There's a policy' . . . all those phrases are excuses for why change can't happen."[1]

Most organizations have trouble figuring out how to use new technologies in smart ways. Even competitive enterprises feeling pressed to boost productivity and hold down costs have a tremendously uneven record when it comes to using technology. One of the fascinating if often overlooked truths Harvard Business School professor Clayton Christensen has pointed out (in *Disrupting Class* and elsewhere) is that new technologies are often pioneered by new entrants, while older, established organizations tend to be wedded to their routines and are thus less adept at taking advantage of new tools.[2]

Beyond the challenges posed by technology, there are other familiar excuses for inaction on school improvement. Contracts, laws, and regulations intended to solve real problems that existed a decade ago can make it tougher to rethink familiar norms. More troubling, too many decision makers have the unfortunate habit of turning these frustrations into all-purpose scapegoats. As one of the coauthors notes in *Cage-Busting Leadership*, there are three kinds of excuses offered for inert leadership—and each is more readily addressed than is typically acknowledged.[3]

One common excuse for moving gingerly is the collective bargaining agreement (CBA) with unions. However, a 2008 analysis of CBA work rules, teacher compensation, and personnel policies in the 50 largest U.S. school districts found that the majority included much room to maneuver. While one third of the contract provisions examined were clearly restrictive, half were ambiguous or silent when it came to key questions such as teacher compensation and personnel policies—and 15% offered explicit flexibility to school and system leaders, such as permitting them to reassign teachers across schools or alter professional development routines.[4] Mitch Price, a legal analyst with the Center on Reinventing Public Education, noted in a 2009 study of teacher contracts that "a lot of these contractual issues are 'smokescreens' for those people who don't want to do something."[5]

A second common complaint concerns the heavy hand of state and federal regulations. Yet Columbia University Teachers College professor Hank Levin recounts that when the California legislature allowed districts to apply for waivers if they could demonstrate that laws or rules were hampering school improvement, "The vast majority of all requests for waivers were unnecessary."[6] Why? Nearly all the proposed measures *were already permissible under existing law.* Superintendents and boards mistakenly thought their hands were tied or, as Levin observed, someone within the districts was using laws and regulations "as a scapegoat . . . to justify maintaining existing practices."[7]

A third excuse is, "We don't have the money to do that." Indeed, a 2012 survey of over 1,000 instructional and IT staff in schools and higher education by technology provider CDW-G found that 88% saw challenges to moving away from the traditional lecture model—with a "lack of budget" named as the biggest roadblock.[8] Yet districts rarely prune staff or programs, even when a new product or service might enable nine employees to accomplish what once took 10. The result: Labor-saving technologies or services rarely appear cost-effective. Larry Berger, CEO of Wireless Generation, has explained that districts too often look skeptically upon products that save teacher time. When trying to sell a handheld diagnostic software tool that could enhance assessment and give teachers better information, saving teachers more than 20 hours a year, Berger kept trying to explain to districts that this would pay for itself—that saving teachers 20 hours a year was like cutting the cost of instructional personnel by nearly 2%, which would more than offset the up-front cost. In response, he found widespread disinterest. The problem? Officials told him that they had no way to recapture those savings because that was already spent money. There seemed to be no appetite for rethinking how new teacher time could be best used on behalf of learning, even if dollars could not be saved.

In each instance, leaders can do much more than they think, if willing to challenge convention and look past urban myth. For instance, Patrick Larkin, assistant superintendent in Burlington, Massachusetts, notes, "Schools traditionally haven't done a great job of looking at what they can cut out of their budgets." He says Burlington has made cuts elsewhere so that it can invest in technology. When it comes to procuring iPads, for instance, he explains, "We wouldn't need to invest money in sets of textbooks. If we needed a new social studies textbook for Grade 9 that was, say, 250 kids times a hundred dollars. We're cutting out those expenses."

In the case of foreign language labs, Larkin says, "We had the iPad cart that we had been using the year before. Foreign language teachers got an OK from College Board to do the verbal part of the AP test using iPads to conduct the recording. After that, I asked the foreign language department, 'Do we still need foreign language labs?' The cost was going to be $100,000 or so. They said, 'If we have iPads next year, we'll have a foreign language lab in every classroom [and would no longer need designated labs].' From that standpoint, it was a huge savings."

Mark Edwards, the Mooresville, North Carolina, superintendent we met in Chapter 4, now spends less than $40 per student *per year* on content, by combining technology-delivered materials and adequate open-source materials. This has helped free up the resources that have fueled Mooresville's remarkable success, despite the system being one of the lowest-spending districts (per pupil) in the state.[9]

TECHNOLOGY IN THE REAL WORLD

Now, there's no use being naïve. While some enthusiasts may hope that technology will wipe away the frustrating politics of education, most educators know better. K–12 schooling involves spending public funds to educate the public's children. This means decisions will invariably be tinged with politics. While distance education may alter the role of school boards or teachers unions, the larger truth is that much of the familiar dynamics of schooling aren't going anywhere. This means that learning engineers need to address those, work with them, and not settle for wishing them away.

What Teachers Think

Like most anyone else, teachers are amenable to new technology when it's comfortable, supplemental, and not disruptive. The evidence also suggests that younger teachers are more likely to be comfortable with new technology and to use it in classrooms.[10] Teachers generally react warmly to technologies that better enable them to share ideas with other teachers or interact with parents.[11] Unfortunately, any meaningful effort to redesign teaching and learning *is* likely to be disruptive, almost by definition. Learning engineers find themselves taking a hard look at work routines, teacher roles, and how time is used.

Many teachers may be skeptical of such changes, and teachers unions have often shown themselves to be fiercely opposed. In Idaho, for instance, the Idaho Education Association (IEA) bitterly fought a legislative package that required students to take online courses and all high schools to provide one-to-one computing in the next five years. The IEA forced a 2012 referendum, on which it spent millions rallying voters to overturn the legislation.[12]

Will Richardson, former teacher and author of *Blogs, Wikis, Podcasts, and Other Powerful Web Tools for Classrooms,* notes the uncertainty that technology can create for teachers: "For us teachers and education leaders, this moment of rapid and radical technological change is not what we signed up for, is it? A trillion web pages; a billion smartphones; movies, TV shows, newspapers, and novels on demand . . . ubiquitous courses and coursework, with teachers, tutors, and technologies that let learners of any age learn whatever they want, whenever and wherever they desire. . . . No, this is not the picture most of us painted for ourselves when we went into education."[13] At the same time, writing in 2013, Richardson advised teachers, "Welcome to what portends to be the messiest, most upheaval-filled 10 years in education that any of us has ever seen. Resistance, as they say, is futile."[14]

In a 2013 nationwide survey of Advanced Placement and National Writing Project Teachers, 75% said that the Internet and other "digital tools" have added new demands and have increased the range of content and skills needed to teach. Meanwhile, 41% say these tools create more work on their part.[15] Jared Covili, who trains teachers to use technology in Utah, says the reactions vary enormously. "It's a mixed bag," he says, recalling a district that purchased an iPad for each of its teachers, "We had some people that opened the iPad for the first time at the training. And we had other people who had been working on it the minute they got it, had it all set up, and were really looking for how they could use it in the classroom."

Michelle Tubbs is principal of Alliance Tennenbaum Family Technology High School, a "blended" Los Angeles charter school. Tubbs has said that one challenge is simply finding teachers willing and able to teach in that new environment. She has lost two teachers over difficulty with lesson planning and working extra hours. Tubbs explains, "They have to learn a different type of classroom management where you look around the room and say, 'I know you are not on Compass Learning for Algebra II because your body language is telling me you are having fun' . . . it's a tough balance." The teachers that do stick have to be comfortable with the school regularly tweaking the model. Tubbs says, "It's action research every day. We are the ones who are pioneering this, so we are the ones who have to be willing to test and try, plan and retest."[16]

Helping teachers learn how to leverage technology in the classroom can be difficult, especially if they have a hard time seeing the value. Jared Covili says he spends as much time explaining how to best use new devices as he does convincing teachers they should use them. He says, "Fifty percent of it is definitely teaching the 'how' and 50% of it is teaching the 'why,' because you've got to do both." Covili emphasizes that it's important to put oneself in a teacher's shoes. He says, "You're already asking me to do so many other things as a teacher. Now, you're trying to revamp my curriculum to bring in technology. . . . I just don't have the time to learn how to do it. And sometimes it doesn't work the first time, and I don't have the time to troubleshoot it and make sure that everything is working."

Naturally enough, union leaders typically seek assurances that technology won't threaten jobs or upend familiar work routines. This can make learning engineers feel that they have to settle for squeezing new tools into old contract language and policy.

One of your coauthors recalls the smartboard demonstration of an interactive virtual curriculum being delayed because union work rules prevented the teacher from plugging the power cord into the wall. Others had been punished for violating these rules, so the teacher adamantly insisted on waiting for the proper support staff to arrive. Any seasoned leader has a raft of similar such tales. It is up to thoughtful administrators, working (one hopes) in tandem with open-minded union leaders, to find ways to rethink these aged rules and rigid routines.[17]

The policy challenges are real. But there are also self-imposed burdens born of the haphazard way in which new technology is often adopted and implemented. There's a temptation to rush ahead "because we can't afford to wait" or because an associate superintendent is wowed by a conference presentation. As one district technology leader observed, "You cannot say, 'Thou shalt integrate tech and Web 2.0,' and then just put it on the teachers. They'll never do it. Teachers are already drowning. You need teachers who have gotten excited about the possibilities and who will go out and show it and support it. Start by focusing on people who embrace it and not on the others who pose you with a losing battle. We focused on the people who embraced it and built excitement. Then, that other 20% will either come along or they won't. If they won't, then you need to get rid of them. Each year, that population of the unwilling shrinks, but you need to be willing to help them get over that or tell them to find another place to work."

Teacher skepticism about technology is well-earned. After all, changes are often introduced without any evidence they'll improve learning. When they don't deliver, teachers are left justifiably leery the next time. Teacher Roxanna Elden, author of *See Me After Class*, has wryly captured several concerns that educators have when it comes to technology. She's written a love letter to "education technology" that is well worth keeping in mind every time a superintendent, technology director, principal, or assistant principal gets frustrated that teachers are balking at some new technology iniative (see sidebar).

THE "COMPLICATED" RELATIONSHIP OF TEACHERS AND EDUCATIONAL TECHNOLOGY

Veteran Miami teacher and author Roxanna Elden has eloquently captured the mixed feelings that teachers have about much hyped education technology. In a 2011 piece for *Education Week*'s "Rick Hess Straight Up" blog, she wrote:[18]

Dear educational technology,

These days, we run into you everywhere. People who say you're just what we need have gone out of their way to introduce you, and are quick to criticize us for not showing more interest. So why aren't we more into you? Well, if you want to win teachers over, you have to understand where we're coming from.

You're not the only one we're seeing. When teachers claim our calendars are full, we're not just playing hard to get. We've probably had several other tech-dates this month, including multiple computer-based reading programs for which we have to herd kids into the school library to use the computers. Each of these probably involves a diagnostic assessment, plus corresponding practice and makeup assessments, each of which requires the library to stay closed for the day, which means kids can't check out any actual books until well into the third month of school, once we've finished assessing why they're not good readers.

We want to know you respect us. Teachers have plenty of experience with products that require two hours of tedious busy work for every hour they "save." During a first impression, we look for signs that innovations in technology are matched by a genuine desire not to waste our time. High-tech isn't always best for this: A 90-minute webcast of an underprepared presenter mumbling through a PowerPoint presentation in another school's auditorium is arguably more insulting than making us sit through a bad presentation in person. If you want to start things off on the right foot, show the same consideration for our needs that you claim your technology does for students.

We've been hurt before. Teachers want products that are user-friendly—and won't leave us feeling used. It will be hard for us to trust you again if we have to find out about password problems in front of our students or troubleshoot during computer-based high-stakes testing. Please, work out your own issues before introducing yourselves.

We get suspicious when you promise us the world. These days, if students were motivated enough, they could get the equivalent of a college education through their smartphones.

Or they could spend all day playing video games and watching porn. Even the best high-tech solutions don't override the bugs in human nature. Kids who struggle with reading will struggle to guide themselves through computerized directions. Cheaters will find high-tech ways to cheat, and students whose printers seem to break the night before every due date will have similar excuses for why they couldn't watch their online lessons when we "flip" our classrooms. Sure we'd like your help, but you'll get farther with us if you don't pretend to be something you're not.

Sometimes the problem isn't you. It's us. Your software is only as good as our schools' hardware, and many schools still have slow computers, or not enough computers, or don't have the Internet capacity to stream videos and interactive lessons into multiple classrooms. Your three-minute video may take five minutes to load on our interactive whiteboard, which feels like 20 minutes in a class full of rowdy seventh-graders. If high-tech lessons take a toll on classroom management or require us to track down the IT guy our school shares with three other schools, don't be surprised if we decide we're just not compatible.

Deep down, we still believe in love. Sure, we've got some trust issues from being burned in the past, but that doesn't mean we're nostalgic for the days of clapping erasers and calculating grades by hand. Teachers have had good experiences with technology, too, and we'd love to have more. The good thing about teachers is if you treat us right, we're loyal, and we'll tell all our friends how great you are. For now, trying to take it slow doesn't mean we're not interested.

We just want to know we can rely on you before we introduce you to our kids.

What are the lessons from all this? First, don't mistake teacher interest for union acquiescence or union resistance for teacher hostility. Instead, work to engage sympathetic teachers in school redesign, while recognizing that some will nonetheless regard many changes as threatening. Second, recognize the checkered history that has fueled teacher skepticism and do your best to use voluntary pilots, phased rollouts, and professional rewards to address these concerns in a serious manner. Savvy leaders seek to ensure the presence of champions in the schools who want to use the new tools and who can reassure and mentor their peers.

What the Public Thinks

The public broadly supports the notion of technology in schools, though it tends to be enthusiastic about "more" technology and less enthralled with disruptive changes. This requires learning engineers to proceed with a careful eye to both educating the public and recognizing what it will and won't accept.

When asked in a 2012 Dell-sponsored survey whether there should be more or less technology in the classroom, 75% of parents said "more" while just 16% said "less." Among both teachers and students, the results were similarly enthusiastic—with 81% of teachers and 74% of students also saying "more."[19] Yet when asked by Gallup in 2011 about high school students "attend[ing] school for fewer hours each week" if they use technology to learn outside of school, 59% of respondents were opposed.[20] In 2012, when Harvard University's Program in Education Policy and Governance asked whether high schoolers should be able to take "approved classes either online or in school," barely half of respondents were in favor.[21] In other words, the public is much more mixed on alterations to the familiar rhythms of schooling than it is on school technology in general.

The public broadly likes the idea of using online classes to provide new opportunities to students in traditional schools who lack them; in 2012, 58% thought students in rural areas should have online opportunities. Fifty-seven percent said students should be able to take advanced courses online for college credit. Online courses for dropouts and home schoolers, however, are much less popular. Just 44% of respondents wanted public funding to help dropouts take courses online; for home schoolers, the comparable figure is only 28%.[22]

It's now pretty much universally held that students need access to the Internet in school: Even in 1996, 80% of respondents said they did. In 2011, the comparable figure was 91%.[23] Meanwhile, support for spending on technology has modestly softened. In 2000, 82% of respondents told Gallup that schools should invest more in computer technology. In 2011, 74% favored additional spending, while 25% were opposed.[24] In short, technology spending remains popular, if less so than a decade ago.

When making sense of all this, learning engineers do well to keep in mind Apple impresario Steve Jobs's take on customer feedback: "It's hard for them to tell you what they want when they've never seen anything remotely like it" and "This is what customers pay us for—to sweat all these details so it's easy and pleasant for them to use our computers."[25] It's up to learning engineers to get learning to work better for all concerned. If they get that right, our hunch is the polls will follow.

Once you get far enough into rethinking with technology, some contingent of parents is almost sure to insist, "But this doesn't *look* like a good school should!" When this comes up, it's good to keep in mind that schools play at least two key roles for families. One is a matter of teaching and learning. The other is serving as a solution to day care and as a community anchor. For many families, the second can sometimes outweigh the issues of teaching and learning, which is why families will fight tooth and nail to keep schools open even when the evidence suggests that kids might be academically better off at another school. Any effective learning engineering solution at scale has to recognize these concerns.

The challenge is to integrate technology in a way that supports good learning practices while respecting competing priorities. Online tutoring can reduce the burden on teachers, while additional coaching and the use of tools like ClassDojo might help support positive student behaviors typically associated with a "traditional" classroom. All of this can still be provided inside a protected learning community for the day, too, ensuring families still have a safe place for their kids.

In other words, there is no necessary contradiction between technology-aided redesign and the assertion that some students need a "traditional" environment. As with books and chalkboards, technology can be a tool for enhancing and extending, rather than replacing. A learning engineer asks how, when, and where we can tackle the day-care and community-institution pieces—and is OK with the reality that those will sometimes trump or circumscribe the range of feasible approaches to redesigning schools and schooling.

WHEN RULES GET IN THE WAY

Rules can and do get in the way. For instance, Digital Learning Now! a group that advocates for digital learning-friendly policies, has noted that quality digital learning requires "student access," "personalized learning," and "quality choices." But barriers to these abound, including state restrictions on access to out-of-state digital content and online courses, seat time requirements, restrictions on the number of credits that students can earn online, and a lack of certification reciprocity for online instructors certified in another state.[26] Addressing these policy impediments is no simple task: it requires equal parts moxie, patience, and creative problem solving. Yet instead of being cowed by frustrating or outdated regulations, learning engineers identify what's in their way and then find a path forward.

Friendly policymakers have a vital role in freeing up schools and systems to rethink old routines, but they need school and system leaders to let them know what needs to change. Most pressing, though, is being clear on these obstacles and starting to think of ways to work through or around them.

Class size in cyberspace: When it comes to online charter schools, many states restrict class size. Arkansas restricts online classes to 30 students per teacher, while California limits them to 25.[27] California stipulates that students can enroll in a virtual charter school only if they live in a county contiguous to where the virtual school is chartered.[28] Imagine the sale of books or music being restricted this way—if a given author or artist could sell downloads to people only in a nearby geographic area, regardless of the quality or popularity of the work.

But these challenges are not insurmountable. When virtual learning provider K12, Inc., ran into California's size limits on virtual schools, the leadership at K12 didn't give up. Instead, it pulled out a map of the state, looked at student census numbers between contiguous counties, and set up a network of virtual charter schools within California to serve almost all students with a small number of virtual schools. Yes, this was a silly waste of time and administrative overhead (every school needed its own adminis-trivia as a separate school, of course)—but that didn't mean K12 wouldn't serve California—it just meant the company had to get creative. That's what learning engineers do.

Seat time restrictions: Some states require a certain amount of in-class "seat time," a decided obstacle for virtual schools—which, after all, *don't have "seats"*! The National Governors Association reports that, while 36 states grant districts and schools some abil-ity to award credits based on mastery rather than seat time, sev-eral only permit mastery-based credits in physical education, art, and health—and not in core courses like English, math, history, and science.[29] For instance, the Illinois school code requires that students have a minimum of five hours per day of in-class instruc-tion, a requirement that blocked plans to establish a full-time vir-tual school in Chicago in 2008.[30] Rather than give up, the founders discovered a way to sidestep the regulation, and instead created the blended VOISE Academy, which combines an entirely online curriculum with in-person teacher supervision.

Dealing with existing laws can require this kind of problem solving. In Wisconsin, for instance, the state law had long defined "schools" as place-bound entities, posing severe challenges to online schooling. In 2007, for instance, a state appeals court had ruled that the Wisconsin Virtual Academy violated state laws because it meant the school board was overseeing a charter school located outside the district, with students attending a school outside the district in which they were enrolled. The court therefore deemed the academy ineligible for state funding. The educators informed legislators of the problem and proposed a fix. The next year, in response, the Wisconsin legislature enacted Act 222, which changed charter school, open enrollment, and teacher licensing laws to allow virtual charter schools to operate with public funding. The new act "specifies that for open enroll-ment and other purposes, a virtual charter school is located in the school district that has contracted for the school's establish-ment."[31] Legislators can be remarkably helpful when presented with fixable problems and straightforward solutions that don't require new dollars.

Spending rules: Funding guidelines can create a variety of headaches for learning engineers. One common frustration, notes veteran education attorney and consultant Melissa Junge, is that federal funding rules can leave districts feeling pressed to "push technology into the classroom without considering how it will be used, whether it is needed, [or] whether teachers and students will know how to use it. . . . The powerful role grant deadlines play in driving this kind of spending often gets overlooked." She explains, "Auditors occasionally cite districts for making large, end-of-year purchases that aren't needed to deliver immediate services to students." She cites one district that was "taken to task" for warehousing 30% of its purchases. Junge observes, "These situations highlight how technology purchases are often a spending strategy" rather than a coherent "educational strategy."

Junge's colleague, attorney Sheara Krvaric, adds, "Federal law sets different rules for different kinds of purchases. Expensive items that qualify as 'equipment' are subject to more oversight than less expensive items that are considered 'supplies.' While technology items themselves usually are not expensive enough to be 'equipment,' they are often bundled together for larger initiatives—putting them into a gray area." Krvaric recalls, "One district got tripped up when it bought different pieces of technology that were going to be used together to make mobile computer labs. The individual items were not particularly expensive—laptops, laptop carts, and so on—but, because they were going to be used together," they required more extensive approval and monitoring.

Tackling these spending questions requires a two-pronged approach. First, it's important to work with state officials to streamline and revisit state procurement policies. Second, it's essential to work with the district procurement team to explore where policies ought to be updated to reflect new technologies and practices to minimize headaches and delays.

Title I: A particular challenge is the array of constraints on the use of Title I funds. Many district leaders would love to use Title I funds to help provide low-income students with crucial tools and supports. However, current regulations are typically understood to mean that such efforts are not permitted if a district is pursuing a *district-wide* technology strategy. After all, the well-intentioned goal of Title I is to ensure that states and districts don't use federal funds to displace other spending, but to add resources for the most vulnerable students. The trick is that this framework doesn't account for the fact that new media, once acquired, can typically be delivered for a set cost to all students—not just to the targeted low-income students. As one district chief information officer notes, "We could use that money to help deal with some of the equity issues [around access to technology]—but, today, because our netbook carts are a district standard at all our campuses, our federal grants coordinator tells me that using funds for tech would be viewed as supplanting [and therefore impermissible]."

Explore whether state officials are interpreting Title I prohibitions too broadly, whether they've fallen into a habit of declaring practices impermissible when they might actually pass muster. Even if the prohibitions are as advertised, there are often big opportunities to work with other districts and friendly state officials to devise workarounds or find ways to read regulations less restrictively. For example, Junge tells of one district that wanted to use Title I funds to implement a Lego robotics program as part of a science, technology, engineering, and math (STEM) push in its Title I schools. The state said that the district couldn't do this, asserting that Title I funds could be used only for reading and math initiatives.

The district didn't just throw in the towel. Rather, Junge worked with district officials to assemble excerpts from Title I statutes and Department of Education guidance to make it clear that Title I dollars can be used much more creatively than the state had allowed. Next, the district articulated the rationale for its decision, explaining how it supported the district's improvement plans and would help boost academic outcomes. Finally, Junge and Krvaric identified other states that permitted districts to use Title I funds in the way the district proposed, so as to "help the risk averse [local and state officials] feel more comfortable that they weren't out there on a ledge." This approach offered state officials a rationale for why it was worth the effort, and reassured state Title I staff that they wouldn't be asking for trouble. The state officials reversed their previous decision and gave the district the go-ahead. Krvaric acknowledges, "It's a slow approach—addressing the underlying legal concerns, addressing the underlying policy concerns, and identifying others who can trailblaze with you—but it can get people to yes."

Keep in mind, notes David DeSchryver, a veteran education attorney with DC-based Whiteboard Advisors, that technology is now "way ahead of the assumptions that underlie [federal] fiscal requirements. This is resulting in frustration for district program and fiscal directors. . . . Title I cannot be used for a program that can provide both supplemental instruction to eligible at-risk students and basic services for non-Title I eligible students. In other words, Title I cannot handle the emerging adaptive instructional technology programs that can and are doing both."[32]

E-Rate: Another program that can create complications is the federal E-Rate program, which spends $2.3 billion a year to extend Internet access for eligible schools and libraries. For instance, regulations allow districts to use E-Rate funds to pay for data plans for students, but only so long as those devices don't leave school grounds. As one district technology official says, "It's great to provide connectivity and access at school, but what about kids who don't have broadband connectivity at home? We issue smart phones to fifth-graders with data plans, with the calling and texting turned off—so they're just mobile learning devices." The funny thing is that such districts don't need a data plan during school hours, because the devices can connect wirelessly to the district system at school. The value of the data plan is really after kids leave the building—yet once students take the devices home they can't connect to the web. OK, maybe "funny" isn't the way to describe this—"Kafkaesque" might be better.

In 2011, the Federal Communications Commission announced the $9 million E-Rate Deployed Ubiquitously (EDU) Pilot Program, to help school systems use E-Rate funds to support wireless connectivity for mobile learning devices outside of school.[33] Twenty districts received funding, including California's San Diego Unified, which used the money to supply middle school and high school students with wireless-enabled netbooks that could be used anywhere.[34] The EDU program resulted from persistent inquiries and advocacy by school system leaders and the ed-tech community. The pilot was designed to help determine whether such services should be "eligible for E-Rate support on an ongoing basis."[35] As Michael Horn and Katherine Mackey of the Clayton Christensen Institute have noted, the federal government is exploring ways to modernize the E-Rate program, "including simplifying its bureaucratic paper work, providing more funds, and creating looser rules."[36] This is precisely the kind of place where proactive district leaders who seek out sympathetic federal officials may find them receptive to providing new flexibility. The program garnered new attention in 2013 when President Obama called on the Federal Communications Commission to increase available funding and improve E-Rate's utility for the growing number of schools pursuing digital learning. It remains to be seen whether and to what extent such changes will manifest.

Many federal and state policies governing traditional school spending are a poor fit for new tools and new school models. Learning engineers should be prepared to find ways to push past the various obstacles that confront them as they seek new solutions.

KIDS WILL BE KIDS

There are many reasons to wonder whether students can be trusted with technology, given concerns about distraction, cyber-bullying, lost devices, and X-rated websites. Heck, students' very acuity with devices may enable them to stir up trouble. As one high school principal quipped to a local news outlet about students and technology, "It's hard for us old fogeys to keep up."[37]

Eric Sheninger, principal of New Milford High School in New Jersey, explains: "There's a [fear] that, if you allow students to use their own devices, all they're going to do is text in class and cyberbully each other. . . . That fear factor really has a profound impact on leaders."

This distrust is pervasive. Patrick Larkin, assistant superintendent of Burlington Public Schools in Massachusetts, says, "There are still a large percentage of schools that don't allow students to bring in cell phones . . . making the jump to having a mobile device in the hands of every student is hard. They're scared about what can go wrong, about negative PR, about bullying. Your school culture is going to be amplified by technology. If you have issues like [bullying], then you have a lot of work to do. But the biggest stumbling block for a lot of these schools is that the leaders are scared."

Lenny Schad, chief technology information officer for Houston Independent School District notes, "You need understanding from everybody in the community to do this, because it is a riskier environment. You encounter discipline issues that teachers never had to deal with before." Speaking about his experience in his former district, Katy Independent School District, he says, "We didn't know for sure what we'd be dealing with. We never let ourselves become afraid when bumps occurred; instead we handed out appropriate discipline and used them as learning opportunities. Now, this requires the school board and superintendent to stand tall when faced with [a] parent concerned about the content their kids are accessing and says, 'This is what my kid accessed on the web.'" Schad observes, "This is the world our kids are going to live in the rest of their lives. We want to prepare kids to live in that world and to be good digital citizens in it."

When it comes to reasonable concerns that students will be irresponsible with school-owned devices, Schad has found the opposite to be true. He says, "The kids treat them like they're gold." Katy uses the same replacement policy as for textbooks: You lose it, you buy the replacement. Schad notes, "When your kids lose a textbook, it costs X. When they lose this mobile device, it's roughly the same price. We did that because the expectation was, no matter your economic status, if your kid lost the textbook, you are on the hook for that. And so we just decided we'd keep costs in that same price range. We haven't had any parental pushback at all."

Students themselves seem to see much room for smarter use of new technologies in schools. For instance, while a 2012 survey sponsored by Dell found that 65% of students thought "we use too much technology in our everyday lives," just just 24% said the same about technology in school.[38] To our eyes, these results suggest that students feel pretty inundated with technology outside of school— meaning one of the things schools can do, along the way, is help students internalize notions of what it means to be a more discreet, responsible, and thoughtful citizen in a digital world. After all, few teachers ban paper and pencils just because students can use them to doodle—or to pen indecent or even threatening notes.

GOING ONE-TO-ONE

A common step in tech-aided redesign is moving toward a one-to-one model, in which a school has a device for every student. The problem is that buying netbooks or laptops for every student can be unaffordable, especially when figuring in the cost of devices, support, and data plans, not to mention lost and broken devices, updating hardware, and maintenance. It's little wonder that district leaders have been uncertain about how to proceed in an era of tight budgets.

In truth, if tech-enabled redesign requires schools to purchase and service a device for every student, then learning engineers are in for a long slog. The more promising answer is to leverage the hundreds of millions of web-enabled devices that families already own, and then use school-provided-technology to fill in the gaps. As Houston Independent School District's Lenny Schad says, "If districts are taking on all the burdens for these new devices, we'll be at the same place in five years that one-to-one has been for the past 20. The answer is leveraging this tool that everyone has."

There are several familiar challenges that confront one-to-one efforts. One is that not all students have access. Scott Kinney of Discovery Education laments, "There's this mentality that, 'We can't go digital because some kids don't have access at home.' It drives me crazy because, if people don't have access at home and, based on that, you refuse to provide it at school, you're sentencing them to a life of technological illiteracy." Lenny Schad says that district officials complain, "'Only 20% of my kids have devices, so I have to provide them.' That's crazy. The reason they think it's 20% is because they're completely discounting smartphones and [similar] devices that can be incredible tools. I tell them to talk to secondary students at their poorest schools. Seventy percent or more of those students will have smartphones, I guarantee you. Almost every kid has an Internet-enabled device. That is the path to one-to-one."

A second concern is the technical challenges posed by a bring-your-own-device setting where some students have laptops, others have netbooks, and others have smartphones or e-readers. This raises concerns that some students will enjoy unfair advantages and more prosaic questions about how teachers and staff can support all these devices. For one thing, this requires providers to design common platforms that students can access from various devices. For instance, Jay McPhail, chief technology officer at California's Riverside Unified School District, says, "Our online learning management system is pretty much device-agnostic. So as long as those devices can get on the web in any way, shape, or form, that's enough."

McPhail explains: "One place where people get stuck is they think that you're going to have to manage and control technology like you've always done it. And in this environment I don't think you can." Another district chief information officer observes, "The tech department is used to thinking about classroom technology like a light switch—when the switch is flipped, 15 light bulbs turn on. Now, it's more like technology just controls three directly; the others are controlled by students. This means they can no longer provide the same cone of protection or complete control of where students go, who they send to, or what they do online. When it's something like Google Docs, now students are sharing with the world. You can't lock it down in the same way."

Instructive here is the experience of Jay McPhail's district, Riverside Unified, one of the first systems to act after California launched its free digital textbook initiative in 2009.[39] By 2012, Riverside was utilizing 10,000 district-provided e-readers (a mix of Android tablets, iPads, iPod touches, and netbooks). Together with student-owned devices, about three-quarters of the district's 40,000 students had a device in school.[40] McPhail says, "Our kids are carrying this technology in pockets and purses. We used to confiscate it. Now we want them to use it. . . . And we haven't seen a bump either way in terms of discipline [issues] or kids going to inappropriate sites. . . . We want to try and keep kids safe on the Internet. But the way that you keep kids safe is train them to be safe, not fence them out."

Riverside only worries about providing e-readers to students who don't have a device. Even in the lower-income neighborhoods, 60% of Riverside students have smartphones, tablets, or laptops. Meanwhile, McPhail says, the district is saving money on textbooks. For instance, he notes, Houghton Mifflin Harcourt's Fuse Algebra I textbook for the iPad costs $49, compared to a paper price of $120.[41]

McPhail says students are reassuringly careful with school-supplied devices, in part, because they know school officials will confiscate their device if they don't act responsibly (this requires that school officials follow through, of course!). McPhail says the district's loss rate with textbooks was 25%, but the e-reader loss rate is just 5% because the students treasure the devices. One perk, he notes, is that middle and high school students can now take their reading home without having to drag around a stack of textbooks.

SUMMIT PUBLIC SCHOOLS: FINDING A WAY

Diane Tavenner, founder and CEO of Summit Public Schools, in the Bay Area, California, had already built a well-regarded, high-performing charter high school model when she decided to embrace a more tech-infused version in 2011. Founded in 2003, Summit Preparatory Charter High School, Summit's flagship school, scores within the top 10% of schools on California's Academic Performance Index, typically has three-quarters of its seniors pass at least one AP exam, and has seen 96% of its graduates accepted to a four-year college.[42] Summit's six charter schools enroll approximately 1,600 students. Tavenner speaks frankly about some of the challenges that technology-aided redesign brings and how Summit has addressed them.

Tavenner created Summit Prep in 2003 because, after a decade in traditional schools, she'd decided, "The factory model wasn't working." Back then, she recalls, "We adopted every best practice or research finding that we could possibly apply—one subject per year, 100 students, four classes a day, smaller schools, well-trained teachers with 40 days of professional development, personal relationships with adults. And we were highly successful. Yet there were pieces where we felt like we weren't getting where we wanted to be."

In order to be able to offer teachers 40 days of professional development within the standard state funding formula, Summit schools partner with more than 32 different community organizations across the Bay Area to offer two-month career and life exploration experiences and internships in art, photography, and other industries. Tavenner says, "These organizations are totally underutilized during the school day—they serve kids during afternoons, weekends, and evenings." She says, "It was on those kinds of approaches where we cut our teeth thinking outside what the traditional system would say you could do. It took some fancy footwork, but we've been able to do it."

In 2011, Tavenner decided that taking Summit to the next level would require modifying the model. Summit established a partnership with Khan Academy and piloted a self-directed learning model with 400 ninth- and 10th-graders in its two San Jose schools. Students spend two hours each day learning math at a workstation through a competency-based progression supplied by a combination of playlists. Summit used that as an opportunity to provide more time for one-on-one help, teacher-led discussions in breakout rooms, and group projects. Students set their own learning goals, make a plan to achieve them, learn the content, take an on-demand assessment when they're ready, and reflect on their learning and progress.

From early on, Tavenner says, every Summit teacher had a laptop. Every assignment and handout had to be available to parents and kids online. Tavenner says moving this material and information online has been helpful, because, "In the traditional system, a teacher . . . holds all the information about an individual student, and all the power. Even today, it's often in a grade book. If we're lucky, it's in an Excel spreadsheet or an online grade book that only the teacher can see. Even if [parent or student] has the information, they can't do anything about it, because the teacher controls the whole scope and sequence of the course. And all the student gets is absurd feedback midway through the course, telling them, 'Oh, you failed that unit three weeks ago,' when it's too late to do anything about it. When people understand, they see how crazy the old model is."

Students at Summit

Tavenner says the redesign "is consistent with what we've always believed." She says, "The idea is for teachers to spend the vast majority of their time doing high-value work rather than the administrative trivia. We've always had kids build a personalized learning plan, where they want to be in four years—and what we're building now leverages technology to give kids better feedback on goals and help them stay on track."

She points out a number of challenges or obstacles that greet those who pursue technology-aided redesign. One was the initial reaction of Summit's teachers. When the switch was made, she says, "Teachers first had to mourn a little bit because they have this image in their mind of who they are, and now it suddenly looks a bit different. But our model has more of the stuff that teachers got into education for. There's more meaningful one-on-one work, more opportunities to get to know their kids very well. . . . In the traditional model, when we ask teachers to go into the classroom, they have to be really good at a whole lot of things right out of the gate or they're not going to be successful. Now, in our model, teachers can be good at only some parts and still do really well, because they're part of a team [and are supported by the technology]. Previously, they hadn't felt that way."

Tavenner also acknowledges that Summit's self-directed model doesn't work equally well for every student from the outset. She says that, for maybe 20% of the kids, the model "clicks immediately. They're just asking, 'Where have you been my whole life?'" Then, the 60% in the middle need practice until it becomes routine. Tavenner says, "It's harder to learn this way. But within a few weeks they start to get moving, and within a few months they're really moving." Of the remaining 20%, she says, "They were struggling in [the] traditional system, and they're still struggling."

When it comes to getting students onboard, Tavenner says, the key is "lots of repetition. It's about setting goals, making plans to achieve those goals. . . . As the students develop proficiency, they become more comfortable. We get kids who went through K–8, doing OK, and who now see the results and say, 'It seems like I'm not making progress.' We say, 'Right, you're not. You're not learning anything. You're just going through the motions.' That makes for very powerful conversations."

A third obstacle, says Tavenner, is that the policy environment "is not supportive of what we're trying to do. The biggest challenges are around

Students on a Summit campus

seat-time and attendance requirements. We have to take attendance in a certain way to get funded, and the California funding
system is based on age-based cohorts and assessments. In our
model, kids aren't necessarily assigned to a teacher for an hour
anymore . . . so you have to [find workarounds]."

Finally, Tavenner notes that helping parents understand the
value of reimagining the school experience can be a challenge.
She says, "They know the kinds of schools they went to, for better
or worse, and changing that environment is really difficult for
them. Getting them onboard is an ongoing concern. We've done
two things that have helped. First, we explain every single thing
we're doing, why we're doing it, why it's good for kids, and the
research behind it. Second, we've got the kids doing YouTube videos for parents, walking them through what we're doing, and
explaining to parents why this is good and helpful and why they
like it. The kids are really powerful. When we do meetings and the
kids are there, they're incredibly helpful."

The challenges and the obstacles are real. But they can be overcome. Determined, savvy leaders can win over teachers, engage students, woo parents, find ways around rules and regulations, and the
rest. This isn't easy, but Summit (and Rocketship, Mooresville, and
Carpe Diem) show that it is entirely doable.

OVERCOMING THE OBSTACLES

As Tavenner relates, a key reason that technology is rarely used to
rethink teaching or redesign schooling is that it's easier and less
contentious to simply stuff computers into familiar classrooms. Yet
experience has made clear that such efforts don't do much for kids.
If you use new tools to do the same old things the same way, you
shouldn't expect much to change. Keep in mind that leaders can
often do much more than they imagine to overhaul familiar routines or find flexibility in existing regulations and contracts.

For instance, rules *can* be changed so that the definition of
instructional resources or textbooks is altered to include digital
content. In 2009, for instance, Indiana's state board changed the
definition of a textbook to include digital content. This allowed
textbook funds to be used to purchase technology. Former Indiana
State Superintendent of Public Instruction Tony Bennett said that

the aim was to let school systems "reallocate resources toward the delivery model [they] believe to be important."[43] In fact, such rethinking was encouraged.

Mooresville Superintendent Mark Edwards, our friend from Chapter 4, recalls that when he was in Henrico, Virginia, the district was an early adopter of one-to-one laptops.[44] They had to rethink any number of outdated rules to make it work. He recalls asking the state board of education "to move away from procurement regulations requiring that we had to use designated state funding for 'textbooks.' I said, 'Why don't you just say 'curriculum materials' instead?' They made the change, and that opened the door wide." Later, in North Carolina, he says, "There was, I don't want to call it a loophole, but a provision that we could use. I pushed it, and the state, within a year, adopted [our] framework, saying, 'Let's open it up.' We haven't bought a textbook in six years."

Now, *that's* thinking like a learning engineer: clarifying the learning problems that are holding students and teachers back, using all the tools at your disposal to solve them, and finding a path around any obstacles in the way. It's hard work, clearly—but don't let anyone tell you, "It can't be done."

NOTES

1. Corinne Gregory, comment on The culture of "can't" in American schools, *Rick Hess Straight Up Blog,* entry May 11, 2012, http://blogs.edweek.org/edweek/rick_hess_straight_up/2012/05/the_culture_of_cant_in_american_schools.html

2. Christensen, C., Horn, M., & Johnson, C. (2008). *Disrupting class.* New York, NY: McGraw-Hill.

3. Hess, F. M. (2013). *Cage-busting leadership.* Cambridge, MA: Harvard Education Press.

4. Hess, F. M., & Loup, C. (2008). *The leadership limbo: Teacher labor agreements in America's fifty largest school districts.* Washington, DC: The Thomas B. Fordham Institute.

5. Price, M. (2009). *Teacher union contracts and high school reform.* Seattle, WA: Center on Reinventing Public Education. pp. 7, 24.

6. Price, M. (2009). *Teacher union contracts and high school reform.* Seattle, WA: Center on Reinventing Public Education. p. 173.

7. Price, M. (2009). *Teacher union contracts and high school reform.* Seattle, WA: Center on Reinventing Public Education. p. 174.

8. CDW-G. (2012). *Learn now, lecture later.* Retrieved from http://www .cdwnewsroom.com/2012-learn-now-lecture-later-report/

9. *Every child, every day: Mooresville's "digital conversion" puts kids first.* San Jose, CA: Cisco. Retrieved from http://www.cisco.com/web/ strategy/docs/education/CiscoEduEveryLearner.pdf

10. Bill & Melinda Gates Foundation. (2012, February). *Innovation in education: Technology and effective teaching in the U.S.* U.S. Program. Retrieved from http://www.activate-ed.org

11. Purcell, K., Heaps, A., Buchanan, J., & Friedrich, L. (2013). How teachers are using technology at home and in their classrooms. February 28, 2013. Pew Research Center, National Writing Project, and The College Board. Retrieved from http://www.pewinternet .org/~/media//Files/Reports/2013/PIP_TeachersandTechnology withmethodology_PDF.pdf

12. Quillen, I. (2012). Can technology replace teachers? *Education Week.* Retrieved from http://www.edweek.org

13. Richardson, W. (2013, March). Students first, not stuff. *Educational Leadership, 70*(6).

14. Richardson, W. (2013, March). Students first, not stuff. *Educational Leadership, 70*(6).

15. Purcell, K., Heaps, A., Buchanan, J., & Friedrich, L. (2013, February 28). How teachers are using technology at home and in their classrooms. Pew Research Center, National Writing Project, and The College Board. Retrieved from http://www.pewinternet .org/~/media//Files/Reports/2013/PIP_TeachersandTechnology withmethodology_PDF.pdf

16. Headden, S. (2013). The right mix: How one Los Angeles school is blending a curriculum for personalized learning. Washington, DC: Education Sector. Retrieved from http://www.educationsector .org/publications/right-mix-how-one-los-angeles-school-blending -curriculum-personalized-learning

17. Hess, F. M. (2013). *Cage-busting leadership.* Cambridge, MA: Harvard Education Press.

18. Elden, R. (2011, November 7). The relationship status of teachers and educational technology: It's complicated [Web log post]. Retrieved from http://blogs.edweek.org/edweek/rick_hess_straight_up/ 2011/11/the_relationship_status_of_teachers_and_educational_ technology_its_complicated.html

19. Bushaw, W. J., & Lopez, S. J. (2011, September). Betting on teachers: The 43rd annual Phi Delta Kappa/Gallup Poll of the public's attitudes toward the public schools. *Phi Delta Kappan Magazine, 93*(1). Retrieved from http://www.pdkintl.org/poll/docs/pdkpoll43_2011.pdf

20. Bushaw, W. J., & Lopez, S. J. (2011, September). Betting on teachers: The 43rd annual Phi Delta Kappa/Gallup Poll of the public's attitudes toward the public schools. *Phi Delta Kappan Magazine, 93*(1). Retrieved from http://www.pdkintl.org/poll/docs/pdkpoll43_2011.pdf

21. Education Next. (2012). *PEPG survey* [Data file]. Retrieved from http://educationnext.org/files/EN_PEPG_Survey_2012_Tables1.pdf

22. Howell, W., West, M., & Peterson, P. E. (2012). Reform agenda gains strength. *Education Next, 13*(1). 8–19.

23. Bushaw, W. J., & Lopez, S. J. (2011, September). Betting on teachers: The 43rd annual Phi Delta Kappa/Gallup Poll of the public's attitudes toward the public schools. *Phi Delta Kappan Magazine, 93*(1). Retrieved from http://www.pdkintl.org/poll/docs/pdkpoll43_2011.pdf

24. Bushaw, W. J., & Lopez, S. J. (2011, September). Betting on teachers: The 43rd annual Phi Delta Kappa/Gallup Poll of the public's attitudes toward the public schools. *Phi Delta Kappan Magazine, 93*(1). Retrieved from http://www.pdkintl.org/poll/docs/pdkpoll43_2011.pdf

25. Stewart, J. (2011, October 7). How jobs put passion into products. *New York Times.* Retrieved from http://www.nytimes.com

26. Bush, J., & Wise, B. (2010, December 1). *Digital learning now.* Tallahassee, FL: Foundation for Excellence in Education. Retrieved from http://digitallearningnow.com/wp-content/uploads/2011/11/Digital-Learning-Now-Report-FINAL.pdf.

27. Watson, J., Murin, A., Vashaw, L., Gemin, B., & Rapp, C. (2011). *Keeping pace with K–12 online learning: An annual review of policy and practice.* Mountain View, CA: Creative Commons.

28. Izumi, L. (2011, November 18). California impedes digital learning. *The Orange County Register.* Retrieved from http://www.ocregister.com

29. Grossman, T., & Shipton, S. (2012, February 1). State strategies for awarding credit to support student learning. Washington, DC: National Governors Association. Retrieved from http://www.edweek.org/media/23biz-state-1202educreditbrief.pdf

30. Sloan, J., & Mackey, K. (2009, December). *VOISE Academy: Pioneering a blended-learning model in a Chicago public high school.* Education Case Study. Innosight Institute. Retrieved from http://www.christensen institute.org

31. Wisconsin Legislative Council Act Memo. (2007). Wisconsin Act 222: Virtual Charter Schools. Retrieved from: http://legis.wisconsin.gov/lrb/pubs/lb/08lb6.pdf; Watson, J., Murin, A., Vashaw, L., Gemin, B., & Rapp, C. (2011). *Keeping pace with K–12 online learning: An annual review of policy and practice.* Mountain View, CA: Creative Commons. Retrieved from http://kpk12.com

32. DeSchryver, D. (2011, August 25). Technology vs. Title I [Web log post]. Retrieved from http://www.whiteboardadvisors.com/news/technology-vs-title-i

33. Federal Communications Commission. (2011, March 9). Wireline Competition Bureau announces selected applications for the w-rate deployed ubiquitously (EDU) 2011 wireless pilot program. WC Docket No. 10-222. Washington, DC: Author. Retrieved from http://www.fcc.gov

34. Herbert, M. (2011, September 1). E-rate Goes Mobile. *District Administration.* http://www.districtadministration.com

35. Federal Communications Commission. (2011, March 9). Wireline Competition Bureau announces selected applications for the w-rate deployed ubiquitously (EDU) 2011 wireless pilot program. WC Docket No. 10-222. Washington, DC: Author. Retrieved from http://www.fcc.gov

36. Horn, M., & Mackey, K. (2011). *Moving from inputs to outputs to outcomes: The future of education policy.* San Mateo, CA: Innosight Institute. Retrieved from: http://www.christenseninstitute.org

37. Relerford, P. (2007, May 9). The tools to learn—or to cheat; As high schools work more technology into classrooms, they also have to beware of how tools such as phones and MP3 players can be used for cheating. *Star Tribune.* Retrieved from http://www.startribune.com

38. Dell Edu. (2012). *Innovation in education: Public opinion poll of parents, teachers and students.* Round Rock, TX: Dell, Inc. Retrieved from http://i.dell.com/sites/doccontent/corporate/secure/en/Documents/PollOverview_FINAL.pdf

39. Zupp, B. (2011, December 8). Riverside schools point to power of technology in the classroom. Retrieved from http://www.edsource.org/today/2011/riverside-schools-point-to-power-of-technology-in-the-classroom/3915#.UIG_pm_A-M0

40. Zupp, B. (2011, December 8). Riverside schools point to power of technology in the classroom. *EdSource: Highlighting Strategies for Student Success* Retrieved from http://www.edsource.org/today/2011/riverside-schools-point-to-power-of-technology-in-the-classroom/3915#.UIG_pm_A-M0

41. Zupp, B. (2011, December 8). Riverside schools point to power of technology in the classroom. *EdSource: Highlighting Strategies for Student Success* Retrieved from http://www.edsource.org/today/2011/riverside-schools-point-to-power-of-technology-in-the-classroom/3915#.UIG_pm_A-M0

42. Summit Public Schools. Summit Preparatory Charter School: 2010–2011 at a glance. Retrieved from http://www.summitps.org/

43. Mespell, M. (2012, August 16). An iPad for every student; Bluffton High School incorporating technology in the classroom. *Indiana News Center.* Retrieved from http://www.indianasnewscenter.com; Fletcher, G., Schaffhauser, D., & Levin, D. (2012). *Out of print: Reimagining the K–12 textbook in a digital age.* Washington, DC: State Educational Technology Directors Association (SETDA).

44. For more information on the Henrico initiative, see Edwards, M. A., & Wilson, V. B. (2001, May). One size doesn't fit all: Henrico County's alternative programs pave new paths for even its youngest lost souls. *The School Administrator.* Retrieved from http://www.aasa.org/SchoolAdministratorArticle.aspx?id=10852

CHAPTER 7

Bringing It Together

"Rabbit's clever," said Pooh thoughtfully.
"Yes," said Piglet, "Rabbit's clever."
"And he has Brain."
"Yes," said Piglet, "Rabbit has Brain."
There was a long silence.
"I suppose," said Pooh, "that's why he
never understands anything."

—A. A. Milne, *Winnie the Pooh*[1]

Talk of education technology can carry more than a whiff of A. A. Milne's clever Rabbit. There's a lot of Brain out there—overheated, self-impressed conference presentations and dismissive hand waving toward those who just "don't get it." Technology enthusiasts and vendors offer sophisticated, seemingly big-brained promises and plans. They talk in an impressive jargon about technically complex stuff, tossing around references to "immersive environments," "available bandwidth," "hybrid models," and the rest. Indeed, many enthusiasts talk of a "digital revolution" that will sweep away all that we know about classrooms, schools, and systems. Meanwhile, critics fret that new technologies are a threat to teacher professionalism or an assault on the fabric of schooling. Amid all this noise, educators can find themselves uncertain as to what they should make of it all or what's really changed.

We don't know about you, but we find ourselves scratching our heads at a lot of the heated back-and-forth. We've no patience for the notion that education technology is going to magically transform schooling. At the same time, we're befuddled by critics who lament the "invasion" of technology. We can't remember the last time someone seriously suggested that a new X-ray machine or drug regimen was going to render doctors superfluous. Nor can we think of many physicians who complain that CAT scans or lasers threaten to "de-skill" their profession. Instead, when it comes to medicine, we seem pretty comfortable recognizing that technology can provide valuable capabilities but that these are limited—and that new tools are most helpful when they complement and enhance the efforts of skilled professionals.

While we're on a roll, we can't think of many college professors who complain that books have "de-skilled" their teaching—or, alternatively, many reformers who suggest that books are a miraculous substitute for instruction. Heck, while educators once looked askance at the book, today a school that failed to provide books would be regarded as failing to provide the basic tools for learning.

That seems to us the sensible way to think about technology: as a *tool* for learning, one most likely to matter when wielded by skilled professionals.

Meanwhile, a surprising amount of success with education is of the accidental variety, and stands to benefit from the more consistent and purposeful application of learning science. As we've seen, Salman Khan, founder of the Khan Academy, started out by trying to help members of his extended family get better at math without having to personally tutor each of them. He made videos so that he could better leverage his time—yielding a final product that included only his voice-over with a video. It was a happy accident that led to separated audio and visual information, with almost no distracting visuals, a technique shown to accelerate mastery. Meanwhile, by making those friendly, straightforward instructional videos available 24 hours a day, seven days a week, Khan provided an accessible resource for confused learners with nowhere else to turn. The approach is hardly perfect, but it is promising, especially since Khan Academy has solicited feedback, modified its offerings, and begun to run controlled experiments to see what's working and what's not.

Inattention to learning science can lead to missteps and missed opportunities. For instance, many multimedia offerings wind up stuffed with music, videos, or chat boxes, when learning science teaches that less cluttered designs would do more for learning. Intrigued by the enthusiasm for online learning, some college faculty members are now delivering their instruction essentially "as is" to tens of thousands of online participants. Unfortunately, many of these high-powered college faculty members have little or no familiarity with what's known about learning or what that means for education technology.

Peter Norvig and Sebastian Thrun, Stanford University computer science professors, delivered one of these early, incredibly popular online courses. In fall 2011, they taught an online version of their "Introduction to Artificial Intelligence" course—more than 150,000 students started the course (about 20,000 finished).[2] Technology makes this kind of thing possible: The course was affordable (free!), reliably delivered, available 24/7, and capable of being both customizable and data-rich. A terrific start.

In 2012, Norvig delivered a TED talk about designing the course. Some of what he had to say aligns with learning science ("keep the audio informal" and "don't just focus on facts and memorization"), but much that a learning engineer might hope to hear was absent. There was no evidence, for instance, that they tried to systematically tap what research has to say about the value of worked examples or the importance of demonstrations.[3] Now, this is not to particularly criticize Norvig and Thrun—after all, their course features terrific elements, including a better integration of practice than most free online offerings. However, design matters more and more as one's "classroom" gets exponentially bigger— and using a new medium, despite creating fresh opportunities, makes it likely that some old strengths may not translate. The power and peril of technology are that it facilitates the delivery of well- or poorly designed instruction to many more students, more easily, and more rapidly. Educators need to behave accordingly.

Let's be clear about something. Throughout this book we have occasionally sounded critical notes when discussing innovators whom we admire and technologies we value. We do not believe it is useful for learning engineers to be either cheerleaders or cynics. Rather, as with the pathbreaking efforts of Norvig and Thrun, we should value new offerings and possibilities, but with a commitment to constantly asking where innovations fall short, where they're incomplete, or how they might be improved. There *is* a body of knowledge out there to tap—we wish more folks were not *accidentally* doing good work, but *systematically* doing terrific work by taking full advantage of that knowledge.

After all, it's not always clear that fashionable ideas actually tie back to better learning. At the same time, as we've seen, there are schools and systems that illuminate a more promising course and where educators focus on learning design rather than gadgetry. As Kerry Muse, chief learning officer and head of school for Venture Academy, a blended school, explains, "You're not just adding or overlaying technology onto a program that already exists. . . . You have to completely shift what you think about what a traditional class looks like."

Let's return to the physician example: Doctors don't go for quick solutions to surface symptoms. If you went in for a checkup and your physician found high blood pressure, you wouldn't want her to say, "If we drain a pint of blood, we'll have your blood pressure down in no time." We'd call that malpractice. We'd instead expect her to be an expert at using the science to pick from a wide array of technologies to diagnose and help us. We should have similar expectations for technology use in schools.

THREE BIG THINGS TO KEEP IN MIND

As we survey the shifting landscape of 21st century learning, educators are buffeted by a dazzling array of new devices, computer simulations, and portable projects. If we step back, though, we can see these in context, as interesting variations on more familiar themes. Let's take a moment to focus on three broader trends that will continue to evolve in accord with the culture, technology, and the larger economy.

Technology and Teachers

Think back to our earlier discussions of the book. The book freed the teacher from the tyranny of the lecture and the student from utter dependence on his teacher's personal store of knowledge. The impact of this development, though, depended entirely on how capably and purposefully educators and students used these books. A bad book still requires clarifying lectures—and good books help only if students read them.

Technology's impact is minimized when it involves the same teachers doing the same things in the same way as they did before. Think about medical technologies like the X-ray, the stethoscope, or the MRI—advances in medical technology have gone hand in hand with specialized understanding about how best to use them. If doctors equipped with the X-ray machine insisted on still processing the film themselves, their ability to use this new tool to help more patients would be drastically limited. And if those doctors insisted on hand-assembling their own X-ray machines, the whole invention might be seen as an unfortunate distraction.

If students have access to riveting computer-assisted instructional information, demonstration, and "worked examples," the mix of what teachers need to do should change. This entails rethinking a teacher's job description, responsibilities, training, expectations for change and personal growth, and evaluation. If new practices incorporating technology are effective, teachers should be expected to learn and adopt them, just as physicians and medical education are expected to keep pace with new advances and improved treatments.

We need to think differently about how teachers are prepared and supported. It's likely that the skill sets required to teach an online course may look somewhat different from those in traditional classrooms and that therefore support and training ought to vary accordingly. It's hard to say much more on that right now because neither online providers nor training programs have begun to seriously explore what this will require. More fundamentally, whether online or in traditional classrooms, the opportunity for teachers to spend less time conveying content and more time coaching students should have big implications for teacher schedules and duties.

Today's systems for teacher evaluation lean heavily on value-added metrics that evaluate a teacher's impact on reading and math scores. Without wading into the debate about the merits or frailties of such an approach, let's note that these systems work best when one teacher "owns" a class of students for a full academic year. The more teachers are sharing instructional responsibilities, the more students are instructed by online providers, the more tutoring is delivered by someone other than the teacher, and the less rigidly students are organized in traditional classrooms for an academic year, the less these kinds of metrics reflect an individual teacher's performance. This means that state, system, and school leaders will want to reconsider the smartest ways to gauge the performance of individuals or teams.

School and Home

Centuries ago, the introduction of the book enabled teachers and students to "flip" the classroom so that students could learn outside as well as inside a classroom. In important ways, this started to blur the line between school and home. It made it possible for

Abraham Lincoln to (pretty successfully) educate himself on the Illinois prairie and meant that the education of a given student was no longer quite as dependent on the physical presence and quality of the teacher.

Of course, the Internet has taken this phenomenon to a whole new level. Online learning blurs the line between home and school (and even the bus ride between them). It means that learning is no longer anchored to the school building and its resources.

One of us recalls working on the design of a virtual K–2 reading program nearly 15 years ago. At the time, it would have been cheapest just to use one of the popular "basal reading" programs. However, none of those programs made full use of the existing research or technology or really leveraged what could be done in a home environment by an adult working closely with a child. So the development team built an entirely new research-based reading program, one that allowed adults at home to work with students and virtual teachers. The program actually used very little technology for students in K–2, due to their age—the technology was mostly to help the adults to understand the activities they were supposed to do with the students. This kind of blurring of home and school was tougher then but has become increasingly easy thanks to more modern technology.

This profoundly expands the amount of time that children might spend learning in comfortable, personalized settings. If providers design interactive environments with sufficient skill and panache, children can choose to massively increase the amount of time they spend mastering concepts and content from their bedroom, a friend's room, or the local Starbucks. If we just consider the hours that school-age kids spend playing popular video games and find ways to entice them to willingly channel an hour a day of that time into more academically fruitful paths, it could be the functional equivalent of adding perhaps *six weeks* of extra instruction to the typical school year.

This also raises the possibility that disparities in learning will widen between children from educated, more affluent households and those in less fortunate circumstances. If wealthier households have newer, more powerful digital devices *and* take smart advantage of them, the increased availability of digital tools may do nothing to help disadvantaged students catch up to their peers. That's doubly true if more affluent and educated families are those that make the best use of new tools. Such challenges will go unaddressed if we simply place blind faith in the miraculous power of "learning technology." Realizing the full potential of blending home and school for students in the most challenging circumstances will require educators to be at the top of their game.

Data and Competency

The air is full of high-flying talk about data-driven decision making. The truth is that much valuable data often fall short of helping to inform the learning process, even if they serve to evaluate institutions. After all, the once-a-year model of assessment severely limits how much we can learn about what might have helped certain students master a particular set of skills or knowledge. It makes it tough for schools or systems to do much to adapt in a timely or agile manner.

There are vast new opportunities to revamp what it means to collect and leverage data. After all, ventures like Amazon and Facebook are not collecting data on their millions of users once a year; they're collecting that data every minute, using what they learn to constantly tweak their models, algorithms, and offerings. But such a mind-set requires wholly new habits of data collection and use.

Instances of such models are already present in schooling— it's just that they're not widely used. At a place like Florida Virtual School, which is enrolling new students just about every day of the year, the opportunities for continuous learning are radically enhanced.[4] Many of the new university-level free MOOC (Massive Open Online Course) offerings talk explicitly about the vast amounts of data they're collecting, right down to the "clickstreams" the users engage in as they interact. Researchers at the Pittsburgh Science of Learning Center and at Worcester Polytechnic University have begun to use this rich trove of data to look for patterns and problems in online learning, and adjust student activities accordingly.

With the wealth of data that's newly available on student mastery, it's increasingly possible to differentiate learning in systematic ways—even if the teacher isn't a miracle worker. This creates new possibilities for organizing instruction; deploying teachers; and making use of computer-assisted instruction, assessment, and practice. It becomes possible to track student mastery and give feedback to teachers and schools on a continuous basis. Models like the School of One show how students can be assessed and given additional instruction and practice in real time, accelerating mastery and supporting motivation and a sense of efficacy. Places like Mooresville and Rocketship Education arc showing how, even in a relatively familiar brick-and-mortar setting, schools can leverage information, instructional supports, and thoughtful grouping to address students with varying needs in smarter and more customized ways.

EVERY TEAM NEEDS LEARNING ENGINEERS

Getting learning engineers engaged in school improvement can make all the difference, especially when it comes to thorny questions of technology or redesign. For example, a team at Kaplan working on new test prep materials for the LSAT produced an hourlong instructional video for one of the hardest parts of the test, the logic puzzles. (We'll leave the issue of what logic puzzles have to do with becoming a good lawyer to others.) That video seemed like a terrific idea. The video was available on the web, inexpensive to download, and always there—what's not to like?

At that point, a learning engineer got involved. Tapping research on "worked example" problem solving, he worked with the team to design an alternative resource. The team crafted less than 20 different guided problems, basically using low-tech PowerPoint slides—but drawing on learning science. The learning engineer arranged for a quick controlled trial with several hundred online test-takers, comparing the performance of students with no training, those who just watched the video, and those who had the worked-example training.

The result? Students who used the cheaper, quicker worked examples outperformed those who watched the more expensive-to-make, more time-consuming video. Moreover, the exercise shifted the team's focus away from a generic fascination with technology toward the learning research, and it reinforced the idea of rapidly piloting ideas rather than just debating them.

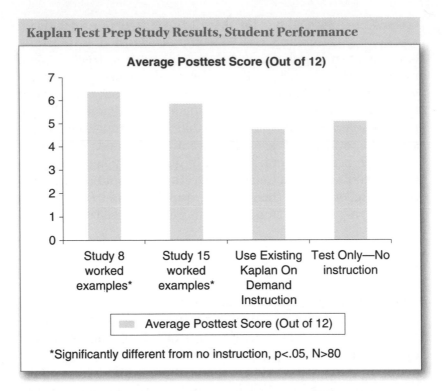

Kaplan Test Prep Study Results, Student Performance

Average Posttest Score (Out of 12)

*Significantly different from no instruction, p<.05, N>80

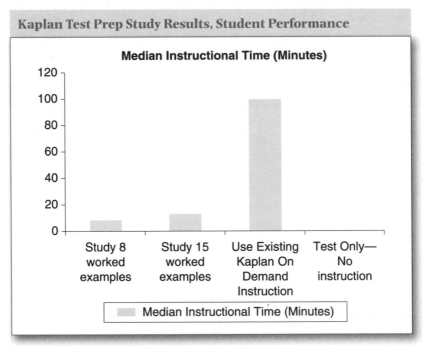

Kaplan Test Prep Study Results, Student Performance

Median Instructional Time (Minutes)

Better learning, less student time, lower cost? That's not a bad combination. But school and system leaders can't do all of this work by themselves. They need to tap learning engineers who can help. Unfortunately, that doesn't mean just turning to a chief technology officer or to information technology staff. Jerry Crisci, director of technology in Scarsdale, New York, explains the risk of just trusting the tech experts alone for this type of redesign: "[T]hings can be driven by the technical needs of the system and not instructional needs." For instance, he notes, "There are some schools that block Google Earth because the IT staff says it is constantly loading data on the map and is going to bring down the network. . . . They're looking at it from a technical standpoint rather than asking, 'How can we use this tool in the classroom?'" He says, "More often than not, when the IT people are running the show, there is less emphasis on instruction than on making sure everything is locked down."

If it's not just turning to the IT team, how can school or district leaders find learning engineers? Keep your eyes open and look around—both inside and outside your school system. One of us works closely with a colleague who spent more than a decade in universities doing controlled trials on instructional design, before moving industries to apply those same principles to corporate training programs.

So such candidates may not be working in schools, or even in a K–12 environment—they might be working at universities, or in workplace training. With the right learning engineering approach, it won't matter— the challenges are similar across a wide range of ages and tasks. (That said, it's indisputable that those designing learning for the littlest students benefit from specialized understanding about their learning, just as pediatric medicine draws on but has essential differences from adult medicine.)

It's an advantage for a learning engineer to have studied cognitive science or learning science, but they really only need to be intellectually agile, able, and willing to read research and ready to try to make sense of the ongoing work at the intersection of cognitive science, "big data," technology, and student learning. Indeed, there are new programs that will take people with instructional design experience and give them a learning science foundation, like the master's degree in Learning Science and Engineering starting up at Carnegie Mellon University in 2013, or the internal training program within Kaplan, Inc., that is meant to give "learning architects" the requisite background in evidence-based instructional design. [5]

OK, so you've got your learning engineer, but you're not exactly sure what to ask her to do or how to tap her talents. Well, here are three easy places to start. If you lean on a learning engineer to help steer just these three things, we think the rest will start to follow more naturally.

Ask how solutions tap learning science: When their wares aren't selling, vendors and developers can be tempted to latch on to cosmetic changes to their offerings or in the marketing materials. This is easier and less disruptive than actually solving the problem. However, if pressed to explain the evidence that these offerings work as intended, providers will have little recourse but to start pursuing more fundamental fixes. This means it's on school and system leaders to ask these hard questions, and demand no-nonsense responses.

Employ smart pilots: When deciding how to employ promising technologies, leaders and their learning engineers should seek to pilot them in a disciplined way. This is tough. It requires a cultural shift, especially in systems where teachers guard themselves against waves of half-baked reforms and faddish new learning approaches. Indeed, too often, interventions are designed with insufficient attention to the rollout, so that teachers have to figure out what the developers should have thought through. Well-designed pilots that include training, monitoring, and coaching of teachers and are linked to good measures of implementation and outcomes can help determine what works and how it can work better.

There's strength in numbers: Scale makes a difference. If learning engineers across many schools or systems collaborate, they can push providers to respond. (Note how energetically publishers and developers have responded to the Common Core State Standards.) Banding together to share data and coordinate pilots can allow participants to learn more quickly which interventions work for which kids. Collaboration enables "research and development" networks that can attract top-shelf research partners, vendors eager to design user-friendly solutions, and funding from foundations and federal research agencies. The federally supported League of Innovative Schools is one such network, but there's plenty of room for more in a nation with 50 million K–12 students.[6]

LEARNING ENGINEERS RIDE IN
THE ENGINE, NOT THE CABOOSE

A common frustration among educational leaders is the sense that online learning and virtual schooling are something being done *to* them by policymakers, their supervisors, and would-be reformers. In our experience, plenty of principals and superintendents feel that they're adopting technology under duress—that the state is requiring them to ensure that high schoolers take at least one online course, and so they've got to make that happen, regardless of readiness or know-how. In other cases, school leaders feel pressed to incorporate virtual school options or to adopt new devices—while remaining unsure how to do it or about the possible benefits for kids.

This is a common challenge. Fortunately, thinking like a learning engineer helps you turn these sorts of mandates into fuel for success.

First, if you regard these dictates as an opportunity rather than a burden, they can be the spark that prompts a reluctant school community to embrace the possibilities implicit in new tools. Once the rethinking begins, a creative learning engineer can help guide the thinking along lines that lead to solving learning problems and not just checking the boxes. Don't settle for layering new technology atop old routines and hoping for the best. Thinking like a learning engineer offers a more fruitful path forward.

Second, thinking like a learning engineer can help you get ahead of these kinds of ongoing mandates. The thing is, many would-be reformers have grown so frustrated with slow-footed or clumsy leadership that they've embraced heavy-handed proposals from above just to get schools and districts moving. School and system leaders are well-acquainted with the results—and they're often not pretty. Consider the case of No Child Left Behind. Though NCLB has some real virtues, including raising the visibility of disparities in student performance, its crude measures of Adequate Yearly Progress and teacher quality and its one-size-fits-all requirements and remedies have drawn the ire of many a school and system leader.

So why did policymakers write such a ham-handed law? Part of the problem was that Congress had come to regard the education community with some suspicion on academic progress prior to 2001. After their fierce opposition to even the modest voluntary testing proposed by President Bill Clinton in the 1994 reauthorization of the Elementary and Secondary Education Act, educators were viewed as naysayers and footdraggers unwilling to help craft workable accountability systems.[7] Leaders would have had a much more prominent place at the table if they were seen as credible, constructive problem solvers.

Foundations, advocacy groups, and policymakers are eager to identify and support savvy, hard-charging leaders and dynamic learning engineers. That's why leaders like Rick Ogston, Mark Edwards, John Danner, and Diane Tavenner are sought out for advice and wooed by foundations. The truth is that legislators, supervisors, and advocates are eager to work with and listen to those they view as no-excuses, practical problem solvers. By showing that schooling can be refashioned by savvy practitioners, learning engineers can temper the sense that external reformers need to "fix" schools through meat-cleaver political policy dictates that can't possibly address the constraints and opportunities that districts face.

Here's the thing. If you, as a learning engineer, turn clumsy mandates into opportunities for smart problem solving, you're doing more than making lemons into lemonade. You're also gaining credibility, making it more likely you'll be consulted or at least get a hearing the next time someone floats a bright idea, and whether it's good or bad, your view of it will be valued. You'll be earning the personal capital that will let you suggest ways to improve current policy without being dismissed as a naysayer.

REVISITING OUR MYTHS

Back in Chapter 1, we observed that educators, parents, policymakers, and the general public can get confused by or caught up in any number of myths when it comes to schools and technology. Some promise that learning engineering is unnecessary if educators will just drink the Kool-Aid and embrace the wonders of the "digital revolution." Others suggest that technology is somehow worrisome or a threat to educators. Let's take a moment to revisit each of these.

Today's kids are different because they are digital natives.
What a kid brings to class in long-term memory today (a dazzling
ability to type on teeny keyboards, for example) is different from
what their parents brought 35 years ago, but the learning challenge isn't. The challenge is still how to help students develop mastery of new knowledge, concepts, and skills. Today's students may
enter school with new things in their long-term memory, but the
fact that learning requires deliberate practice that allows working
memory to build fluent mastery in long-term memory remains constant. Whether students are adept with smartphones or not, mastery is still aided by well-structured information, demonstrations,
deliberate practice, prompt feedback, and motivational support.

More technology yields more learning. This is silly. Sixty years
ago, did having an extra 100 ballpoint pens on hand mean that
students learned more? A generation ago, did having more televi-
sions on campus yield more learning (beyond the plot of *Days of
Our Lives*)? What matters is whether technology is used to
enhance and enrich the key elements of learning—outcomes,
assessments, practice and feedback, demonstrations, information, overviews, and motivation. Technology can help with this,
while making learning more affordable, reliable, available, customizable, and data-rich, but it has to be *designed* accordingly.

Adding technology is "anti-teacher." Technology is not anti-
teacher or pro-teacher, any more than buying your auto
mechanic a new wrench means you're "anti-mechanic."
Technology makes it possible to automate routine tasks, for professionals to spend less time on administrative trivia, and to provide new supports and tools. However, its biggest impact is in
magnifying and extending the impact of terrific teaching. Using
technology to liberate talent from rote and unproductive tasks is a
crucial element of good design. How that plays out in staffing and
job descriptions is an open question and is a conversation that
educators should embrace and help guide rather than fear.

***Virtual schools are "different" from brick-and-mortar
schools, and that's a problem.*** If a virtual school is poorly
designed, that's a big problem. But there's no reason to assume that
a virtual school is inherently any worse than a brick-and-mortar

school. Virtual schools simply pose different constraints (less face-to-face interaction with cheerful peers and caring teachers) and opportunities (less face-to-face interaction with hostile peers and disinterested teachers). A given student may suffer without traditional interaction with peers or in-person time with a teacher; another student may benefit from more customization, a greater variety of course options, and the chance to move at her own pace. Blanket judgments are less useful than an examination of how schools meet the learning needs of their students.

There's "not enough" technology to drive transformation. Sometimes, a leader will explain that learning technology hasn't mattered yet but will once they have enough devices to permit a one-to-one model. Color us doubtful. From a learning engineer's perspective, this makes no sense. Going to one-to-one computing doesn't mean learning will occur—it can provide a solid platform for terrible learning solutions or for good ones. What matters is how learning activities change, how the data flow, or what students do differently to draw on long-term memory for working memory challenges. There might not be enough technology—or there might be too much, consuming too many resources (cash and distracted eyeballs) that would be better directed elsewhere.

The next generation of technology will make things different. There's no particular reason that a student's learning will improve merely because cool, new devices emerge. Heck, we've been hearing this one since the 1980s, and it hasn't happened yet. If you know what you're doing with current technology, then new and improved versions will probably help. But if you don't know what you're doing with today's technology, it's a mistake to put too much faith in the miraculous power of tomorrow's—whatever the Silicon Valley marketing brochures say.

Learning doesn't always work the way we wish it did. Learning is defined by how minds actually work, and that's what learning science can help explain. Nothing we've just said cools our ardor about the potential of technology to profoundly improve teaching and learning. But the next time you hear these familiar myths, just be sure to push past the talking points and focus on what matters.

THE BAD NEWS . . . IS THE GOOD NEWS

Given the pace of change, how can educators keep up and make the right decisions about technology? Fortunately, things are made easier for educators because the way learning works is connected to how our brains are wired. And our brains change a whole lot more slowly than technology.

We closed Chapter 1 by comparing education technology to a rushing river filled with shiny (dare we say sometimes "fishy") ideas. An engineer doesn't just wade in and start grabbing. The engineer thinks it through, erects a bridge from which to survey the river, and baits his hook deliberately. When it comes to schooling, that bridge is learning science. That bridge permits educators to survey the glittering, eye-catching ideas that flash beneath, and choose deliberately. If it's not clear how a given idea will improve teaching and learning, let it pass. If it looks promising, fish it out. You may throw it back, but it's worth a look. All the while, you're not splashing around but are coolly assessing possible solutions with an eye to what matters.

As learning science and technology advance, new possibilities will keep emerging, creating new opportunities to support great teaching and learning. Leaders who possess an understanding of learning science and who have cultivated the ability to diagnose and rethink learning problems will be equipped to leverage new tools, seek smarter solutions, and transform schooling to reliably improve learning over time.

In the end, as we said at the outset, the good news and bad news for digital learning is the same: The solutions with the most evidence haven't been applied yet. The bad news is that this means that learners and teachers aren't benefiting. But the good news is that all these important, well-supported ideas are just waiting to be used.

The United States is a hotbed of innovation across many industries—and nations like China, India, and Japan study our schools as assiduously as we study theirs. Indeed, with the right kind of support and rethinking, the American educational system has enormous advantages when it comes to learning engineering: increasingly sophisticated and coordinated assessment and data systems, decentralized authority leading to multiple lines of innovation, and our historic openness to new ideas and new solutions.

It will require a degree of thoughtful discipline that's often absent, if all this effort is to amount to more than fresh waves of faddism. When it comes to education technology, we'd do well to cease being quite so starry-eyed, especially as we resist the tendency to simply stick with familiar routines. It can be hard to find that sweet spot, especially in a profession that's inevitably whipsawed by moral urgency and frustrating bureaucracies. And that's where learning science can help. Indeed, what Carpe Diem, Mooresville, Rocketship, or Summit teach is that learning engineers can triumph whatever the circumstances and challenges.

The work is doable, and it's essential. It's time to get on with it.

NOTES

1. Milne. A. A. (2005). *Winnie-the-Pooh* (reissue edition). New York, NY: Penguin/Puffin.
2. Kolowich, S. (2012, January 24). Massive courses, sans Stanford. *Inside Higher Ed*. Retrieved from http://www.insidehighered.com.
3. Norvig, P. (2012). The 100,000-student classroom. TED talk. [Video file]. Retrieved from http://www.ted.com/talks/peter_norvig_the_100_000_student_classroom.html
4. *Raising the bar: How education innovation can improve student achievement*. (2013). Hearing before the Subcommittee on Early Childhood, Elementary, and Secondary Education, House of Representatives (testimony of Holly Sagues). Retrieved from http://edworkforce.house.gov/uploadedfiles/sagues_testimony.pdf
5. Learning Science and Engineering Professional Masters Program—Admissions. (2012). Carnegie Mellon University, Human Computer Interaction Institute. Retrieved from http://www.lse.cs.cmu.edu
6. To find out more about the League of Innovative Schools, visit http://www.digitalpromise.org
7. Taylor, W. M., & Rosario, C. (2009). *National teachers' unions and the struggle over school reform*. Washington, DC: Citizens Commission on Civil Rights. Retrieved from http://www.newrochelletalk.com/system/files/Natl+Teachers+Unions+and+the+Struggle+Over+School+Reform.pdf

Index

Figures are indicated by f following the page number.

CORWIN
A SAGE Company

The Corwin logo—a raven striding across an open book—represents the union of courage and learning. Corwin is committed to improving education for all learners by publishing books and other professional development resources for those serving the field of PreK–12 education. By providing practical, hands-on materials, Corwin continues to carry out the promise of its motto: **"Helping Educators Do Their Work Better."**